Successful Living

A STUDY OF BIBLE-BASED ECONOMIC AND LIFESTYLE PRINCIPLES

For Group Study or Personal Contemplation

by Luke S. Weaver

Successful Living

A Study of Bible-based Economic
and Lifestyle Principles

Library of Congress Number: 2010932627
International Standard Book Number: 978-1-60126-246-2

Printed 2010 by
Masthof Press
219 Mill Road
Morgantown, PA 19543-9516

Table of Contents

DEVELOPING BIBLE-BASED ECONOMIC AND LIFESTYLE PRINCIPLES

Acknowledgements v
A Brief History of the Origin of This Book vi
Introduction vii

1. The Right Frame of Mind 1
    - Scriptural Economic Outlook
    - Facts and Attitudes about Money
    - Compliance to God's Ultimate Control
2. The Christian Witness by Lifestyle and Business Manners 16
3. Starting Out Right 21
4. Family Involvements and Interactions 31
    - Necessity and Blessings of Unity in Marriage
    - Including Your Children
5. Neighborhood Relationships and Conduct 43
6. Responsibility, Accountability, Self-discipline and Diligence 49
    - Record Keeping
    - Training Your Family to be Responsible
7. The Work Ethic 67
8. Considerations for Employers 78
9. Instructions for Employees 84
10. Self-Employment 91
11. Thankfulness, Gratitude, and Contentment 93
    - Finding Fulfillment
12. Giving and Other Benevolent Deeds 100
    - Sharing and Helping
    - Hospitality
13. Saving and Investments 112
14. Thrift 118
15. Budgeting 121

16. Responsible Spending 124
Understanding Priorities
Spending with Wisdom and Control
17. Temperance 134
18. Business Ethics and Values 137
Partnerships
Being in Business
19. Lending and Borrowing 148
Debt
Debtors
Credit Card Use
Getting Out of Debt
Creditors
Co-Signing Notes
20. Government Issues and Taxes 156
21. Dealing with Success and Failure 161
Concerning Success
Concerning Failure
22. Insurance and Safekeeping 168
23. Coping with Injustice and Lawsuits 173
Coats, Cloaks and Stolen Goods
Going to Court
24. Warnings about Envy, Greed, and Covetousness, Etc. 177
25. Retirement and the Sunset Years 184
26. Preparing for Your Departure 188
27. Facing the Future 193

About the Author 201

Acknowledgements

This book is dedicated to any and all people who desire to learn more of God's order for life on the earth and how to live a life that is acceptable to the Lord our maker, especially as it relates to lifestyle, financial and business issues.

Credit for the fruition of this book belongs to many people. Much tribute is due, first of all to my own father who endeavored to teach and exemplify truth, virtue, and integrity as he understood it according to the Bible. Though he acknowledged that he was not faultless, he did succeed in leaving a heritage of examples and illustrations of biblical wisdom and common sense knowledge for the family. He taught us many things by telling and re-telling quotes, stories and happenings that illustrated lessons to be learned. Many things were established by specific Bible verses and accounts in the Bible.

There were also other relatives and men around whom I grew up or worked for, from whom I learned many valuable principles in various ways.

Much credit and thanks also belong to the many people who shared personal experiences, thoughts and ideas, and their understanding of the Scriptures.

Thanks also to all those who encouraged the writing of this book and gave suggestions and support in numerous ways. A compliment is due also to all those who helped with proof-reading and other assistance.

This book is not targeted toward specific persons, age groups, types of people, or particular circumstances of any people. The sole hope of the author is that it might serve as a help, or an encouragement to any and all readers in whatever way possible as each one makes his way through this life as a Christian. And may God receive the praise and the glory.

One more acknowledgement is in order. This book quite likely contains some mistakes, misquotes, perhaps some scripture misapplications or incorrect interpretations; or other errors. Readers are free to differ with any issues that are the writer's personal opinion and are at liberty to discuss the matter with whomever they might be studying this book.

Also, any reader is free to communicate with the writer about any issues or necessary corrections.

Luke S. Weaver
31 Rapp Road
Fleetwood, Pa. 19522
email: lukesweaver@gmail.com

A Brief History of the Origin of This Book

In 1992, the author was involved in a discussion with others about the fact that many young people appear to start out in life with insufficient financial direction, and deficient biblical economic wisdom, for a smoothly functioning Christian life-style. Therefore many young men were said to be seriously indebted, possibly from day one, and many are soon in a financial struggle.

Consequently the author was inspired to seek a way of preventive measures to help young people avoid financial problems, rather than needing to find ways to help them after they are already in trouble. The first endeavor was a group of thirty-two questions. They were drawn up by inspiration, with the youth group in mind. It was an effort to stimulate group discussion and open the way for leaving encouragements for the youth to seek direction from the Bible for their way of life, work and business activities.

These questions were addressed and discussed in a mid-week Bible study meeting at church. Interest and participation by the youth was very good. Soon afterward some younger married couples showed interest to do the same. Later some of the parents also expressed interest, and several congregational meetings resulted. From there interest spread among other church congregations for teaching, which eventually resulted in a number of years of lecturing in various places in the U.S. and Canada.

In the course of the lecturing, many topical scripture references and notes accumulated in a note book. Over a period of time numerous people began to suggest and request that the accumulated material be made available in a book. With the passing of time, and after considerable counsel, this type of a study and discussion book seemed like a good thing to do.

The author's hope and wish is that this book might prove to be a help to many people, and a blessing to families and friends, all in a way that will bring honor and glory to God.

Introduction

This is not a "get rich" seminar. It is not a guidebook with detailed formulas or step by step assignments for living. Hopefully though, you will gain some knowledge that will help to make your life function in an orderly way, so that God can bless you and those around you. Also, hopefully there will be some things that will aid you in coping with frequent problems, difficulties, or seemingly unfair circumstances that arise in normal everyday life.

Keep in mind, as you study, that there is no such thing as total financial security, but financial stability should be attainable for most people under normal circumstances. Let this be among your goals of Christian virtues, to find joy in living a God-sanctioned life, marked by economic stability.

This study will not touch nearly every area and circumstance of life; and you may have questions or needs never mentioned in this study; so let God, by the Holy Spirit, speak *your language* to you, for your circumstances, as in Acts 2:7-11, when every man heard in his own tongue.

Because many of the subjects are intertwined, some thoughts and scripture references appear under more than one heading.

We can become so used to a certain way of living that we don't even consider if perhaps we should make some changes in our lifestyle, business manners, or our goals. We might have our minds closed to the possibility of a necessary course correction. As you study, try to be ready and willing for direction from the Holy Spirit for your life. God might want to change someone, "from a stick to a flute," and that change might require some mental discomfort or even pain.

Remarkable progress and improvements are possible, *if* we are willing to be helped. It is wise never to say, "That's not possible for me"; or, "I could never do this or that." Don't underestimate what the power of God and honest commitment to His directives can do in your life.

Not all the points of teaching will apply to everyone or to all circumstances. For instance, some people may need to tone down their material efforts and involvements, and others may need to become more diligent in their labors and business to be in God's order.

Except for the scriptural quotes included, this book should not be considered as final authority on any issue.

Do your best to hang on to, and utilize any points that fit your life and your particular need. Even if you only get one point, God can add His blessing if you put it to practice.

The questions in this study are meant to activate the mind and generate discussion. All participants are encouraged to ask questions and share their input and experiences. Have your Bible available as you go to study because some of the scripture references, especially the more lengthy ones are not quoted. Also, you might want to look up and quote some scriptures of your own inspiration or question.

As you read, study, and discuss, be careful about forming opinions and judgments about the management and finances, or lifestyle and practices of others. Although they might be in need of correction, their circumstance might be much different than you think. The main aim should be to gain spiritual direction and fortitude for your life.

Setting the Right Frame of Mind

CHAPTER 1

"God who made the world and all things therein, seeing that He is Lord of heaven and earth, dwelleth not in temples made with hands; Neither is worshipped with men's hands, as though He needed any thing, seeing he giveth to all life, and breath, and all things; And hath made of one blood all nations of men for to dwell on all the face of the earth, and hath determined the times before appointed, and the bounds of their habitation; That they should seek the Lord, if haply they might feel after Him, and find Him, though He be not far from every one of us: For in Him we live, and move, and have our being" (Acts 17:24-28).

This scripture already goes a long way in guiding our thinking to a proper mind-set. It sets the record straight that heaven and earth and spiritual and natural issues are not separate subjects. God made it all and is still ruler of all things. The Christian, who maintains a vision of *a better country* to come, has a decided advantage in keeping his balance concerning money and other earthly things.

SCRIPTURAL ECONOMIC OUTLOOK

The word economics has a meaning far beyond acquiring and using money. It is "the science that deals with the production, distribution, and consumption of wealth, goods and services." In this study we want to take a look at it from a Bible perspective.

Economic concerns are, to an extent, a secondary subject. For Christians, the first and foremost must be the pursuit of the kingdom of God through His Son, Jesus (Matt. 6:30-34). All else must fall in line *behind* this pursuit. Economic issues and lifestyle choices, though, are not a separate or stand-alone subject. A faith that is alive will affect your everyday life.

1. Often people's lifestyle ideals and the choices they make about acquiring possessions seem to be very closely associated to their financial status and means. Is this acceptable for Christians? If not, why not? If yes, to what degree?

The vast number of scriptures about these issues shows that God does care what is important to us. He cares how we live and do commerce, and how we relate to our families and neighbors. It is important how we treat business people when we're buying; or our customers when we're selling, and a host of other things. God does have a right to be concerned how we think about the things of the earth.

2. How should this realization make us think and feel?
3. Are you willing to be "quickened" in your actions and opinions about the things of this life and the way you live?
4. How does Psalm 14:2-3 apply to our mind-set about earthly things?

There is much direct teaching and many matter-of-fact references in the Bible about money, business and lifestyle. The Bible has an abundance of intelligent advice for finding our way through life. It has been said that Jesus taught more in volume about the earthly life, earthly possessions, and attitudes concerning money and its use, than any other subject.

5. Do you think that is true? Or can this perhaps be answered better at the end of this study?

It is necessary to consider all the scriptures and their context. If one reads only Luke 6:20, "Blessed are the poor"; and Mark 10:24-26, about trusting in riches, the camel and the eye of a needle; and other similar scriptures; then one could conclude that wealth is evil and that poverty assures righteousness.

On the other hand if we read only scriptures like Proverbs 10:22, "The blessing of the Lord, *it maketh rich*"; or Luke 18:29-30, "There is no man that hath left house . . . for the kingdom of God's sake, who shall not receive *manifold more in this present time*, and in the world to come life everlasting"; or the well wish from 3 John verse 2, "*that thou mayest prosper* and be in health;" or the promise of prosperity in Psalm 1:3, "his leaf also shall not wither; and *whatsoever he doeth shall prosper,*" we could get the idea that faith and righteousness guarantee wealth and health. Neither conclusion would be correct in itself. Some scriptures emphasize one point, some another.

6. What then is required to be balanced in our understanding of God's will for us and our families?
7. Is this one of today's biggest tests for Christians?
8. Is the challenge of finding material balance equal for all generations, countries, cultures and eras?

Psalm 1 has much to say about the consequences and outcome of a person's life based on one's choice of virtue and values.

"Blessed is the man that walketh not in the counsel of the ungodly, nor standeth in the way of sinners, nor sitteth in the seat of the scornful. [2]But his delight is in the law of the Lord; and in his law doth he meditate day and night. [3]And he shall be like a tree planted by the rivers of water, that bringeth forth his fruit in his season; his leaf also shall not wither; and whatsoever he doeth shall prosper. [4]The ungodly are not so: but are like the chaff which the wind driveth away. [5]Therefore the ungodly shall not stand in the judgment, nor sinners in the congregation of the righteous. [6]For the Lord knoweth the way of the righteous: but the way of the ungodly shall perish."

The leaf, (or leaves) in verse three can be likened to the daily activities and behavior of our lives. In the natural sense; those who work with fruit-bearing plants know that when there is a problem, the first sign of trouble usually shows up in the leaves, i.e. wilt, curling up, black spots, white spots, holes, brown edges, and other problems. For the plant to yield good fruit, the plant and its leaves must be kept in good health. In like manner, as a Christian, the upright person's "leaf," or his life conduct, should not wither, nor get black spots, etc. The leaves of the everyday life need to be healthy in order for a person to bear fruit to the glory of God.

9. Can we conclude then, that if a Christian is in soul-trouble, some of the first evidence will be in the "leaves:" one's attitudes about

the things of this life, or in the daily round of earthly business, or perhaps a breach in integrity, or erroneous lifestyle choices, etc.?

10. To what degree can a Christian claim the promise in verse 3, that whatever he does will prosper?

Following is a quote from the booklet, *Christian Stewardship in Estate Planning*, by Gospel Publishers. The opening sentence says, "So important is the far-reaching responsibility in material stewardship that Christ placed it as an indicator of our faithfulness in spiritual or eternal matters."

This statement refers to the requisite for Christians to be "faithful in that which is least." Jesus said, "He that is faithful in that which is least is faithful also in much: and he that is unjust in the least is unjust also in much. If therefore ye have not been faithful in the unrighteous mammon, who will commit to your trust the true riches? And if ye have not been faithful in that which is another man's, who shall give you that which is your own?" (Luke 16:10-12).

In these verses the emphasis is on faithfulness, not on intense money consciousness, nor even on quantity of money. Take notice of the word *also*: if a person is faithful and trustworthy; or unfaithful and undependable in little, he will tend to be that way also in much.

11. Because man has a depraved nature, it is not difficult to understand how unfaithfulness in little things will readily show up in bigger issues; but how can the opposite, faithfulness in little things showing up in bigger issues, be true with our depraved nature?
12. Can a person be unconcerned and slothful in earthly things but fervent in spiritual life?
13. Is it true that if one is careful and diligent in the smaller things, the big things will tend to take care of themselves?
14. Concerning faithfulness in that which is another man's (v 12), how can parents best train their sons and daughters in the necessary qualities of honesty and trustworthiness to prepare them for faithful service, especially when it involves other people's money or things?
15. In what way does this training affect the making of a future deacon, or a deacon's wife?
16. When should this training start? How?

Luke 16:13 continues, "No servant can serve two masters: for either he will hate the one, and love the other; or else he will hold to the one, and despise the other. Ye cannot serve God and mammon."

It has been said that you can serve God with money, but you cannot serve God and money.

17. What's your input?

Following are a few examples concerning the gravity of financial faithfulness. A certain man, as he searched for God and peace, became convicted about how unfaithful he had been as a steward and how he had wasted his money. This became a major part of his repentance experience, and he became convinced that God surely cares about how we use our money and possessions.

Another man took a new job. One day soon after he started this job, he gleefully told his boss about a shrewd deal he had pulled off, and how much extra profit he had made for him by doing it. Instead of rejoicing about the deal, his boss promptly dismissed him. He told him that he could not use him because an employee who would steal for him would also steal from him, and he would have no part with cheating or stealing. This account also illustrates unfaithfulness with another man's money.

Paul wrote to the Corinthians about mandatory faithfulness. "Moreover it is required in stewards, that a man be found faithful". (1 Cor. 4:2).

18. What generates genuine faithfulness?

How you are presently managing your own affairs says lots about you and whether or not your church or mission board could trust you and your children to be faithful with church or mission funds. Responsibility can sometimes rapidly change a person's behavior; normally, however, it will not automatically change a person for the better. As a rule, the proper qualities must be learned at home.

19. Is it fair then, to assess a person's eligibility for service by their financial circumstances or one's conduct with their own money and possessions?

Sunday is a special day for Christians, but your conduct on the other six days of the week shows who you really are, and what your faith is doing or not doing for your life. Your demeanor on the other six days is six times as important as Sunday. That is when you make your mark in society. That is usually when you will have the strongest influence on those around you, for better or for worse, depending on what you are at heart. John 15:8, "Herein is my Father glorified, that ye bear much fruit, (every day of the week); so shall ye be my disciples."

20. How concerned and conscious should one be about the influence their lifestyle and daily conduct has on others?
21. Is it possible to have a neutral effect on others and make no marks in society?
22. When do young people become responsible for the effects of their actions and attitudes?

People, their temperaments, and circumstances are different from each other; in fact, it appears that God does not intend for all people to be and do alike. But the Bible principles are always the same, for every nation, culture and era.

"Forever, O Lord, thy word is settled in heaven" (Ps. 119:89). "The grass withereth, the flower fadeth: but the word of our God shall stand for ever" (Isa. 40:8). People come and people go (they wither and fade away), times change and conditions vary, but Truth is always constant and reliable.

23. How is this possible, that "one book fits all," and always?

FACTS AND ATTITUDES ABOUT MONEY

Money is a neutral medium of exchange, a system of regulating trade. It is neither good nor bad in itself. But, how people feel about it, the love of it, the many negative ways and means by which people get it, and what they do with it; these things can and do cause many and huge problems for humanity. Money can give feelings of elation, but just as readily it can cause much anxiety, grief, violence and suffering. Because money represents wealth, power and status, there is a big danger of being overtaken with an excessive desire to succeed and excel.

1. Can you quote some scriptures to help keep a proper perspective about money?
2. Can you name some common sense factors to follow, to stay balanced in this issue?

Money cannot buy love, happiness, friendship or peace, but a love for money can certainly kill these virtues. Winners of large lotteries and persons who suddenly fall into great wealth often discover this fact. Many people who have sought fulfillment by wealth and possessions have had much trouble and deep disappointment.

1. What are some good ways to come to grips with the propensity to equate happiness with riches?
2. Does the book of Ecclesiastes help?

Money actually is very limited in what it can do for us.

"Money can buy the husk of many things, but not the kernel. It brings you food, but not appetite; medicine, but not health; acquaintances, but not friends; servants, but not faithfulness; days of joy, but not peace and happiness (Henrik Ibsen 1828-1906).

"Look to your health; if you have it, praise God, and value it next to a good conscience; for health is the second blessing that we mortals are capable of; a blessing that money cannot buy. (Izzak Walton 1593-1683).

Make no mistake; every good gift comes from God—not from money. See James 1:16-17.

3. What does it take to acquire an understanding about the limits of money?
4. If money is in fact so limited, why then does it say in Ecclesiastes 10:19, that *"money answereth all things"*?

First Timothy 6:10 says "the love of money is the root of all *(kinds of)* evil." It is truly so, that a love for money causes every imaginable kind of troubles and problems among people.

Also Ezekiel 7:19 mentions that the people's silver and gold, their money, was "the stumbling block of their iniquity." It sounds like it was their money that caused them to stumble into sin.

It seems that a wrong attitude about money can give it a strange and astounding power over people and cause them to do things they had not planned on.

1. It's not money that's the problem, but the love of it that brings trouble. True or false?
2. What is the best defense to keep from being brought under the power of money?
3. If we could comprehend the real truth about riches, would money lose much of its appeal?

A much-used word of caution among Christians and even in secular society concerning imbalance in the things of this earth is *materialism*. A dictionary definition for this word is "The theory or doctrine that physical well-being and worldly possessions constitute the greatest good and highest value in life; a great or excessive regard for worldly concerns." The first definition would be raw materialism. The second meaning, about excessive regard . . . might often be less obvious in life. First Timothy 6:5 refers to another kind of materialism, "supposing that gain is godliness." A sober concern about this issue is very much in order.

4. There may be many types and varying degrees of materialism. Are they all wrong?
5. How would you define "excessive regard for worldly concerns"?
6. What is the answer for overcoming this problem?

A problem closely related to materialism is that of a mind already busy with other interests when God calls for one's attention. It is called preoccupation. A dictionary defines it as "The state of being preoccupied; absorption of the attention or intellect. Something that preoccupies or engrosses the mind: *Money was their chief preoccupation.*"

This is not just a current-day problem. We find an example of this in Matthew 22: 4-5: "Again, he sent forth other servants, saying, Tell them which are bidden, Behold, I have prepared my dinner: my oxen and my fatlings are killed, and all things are ready: come unto the marriage. But they made light of it, and went their ways, one to his farm, another to his merchandise."

The tendency to be more concerned about material things than spiritual things is not limited to any group of people. Those who are well to do; those who have an average and adequate living; and those who have very little can all have an acute case of materialism.

7. Is the answer to this problem the same for everyone: the more well to do, those in the middle, and those who struggle to make things work?
8. Can you quote a scripture that has the answer for this human inclination?
9. Is the prayer in Proverbs 30:7-9 an adequate answer?

Money and things are only for time on this earth. Second Peter 3:11 says, "Seeing then that all these things shall be dissolved, *what manner of persons ought ye to be in all holy conversation and godliness?*"

10. Can you answer this question?

In 1 Corinthians 7:30, Paul wrote about one's mind-set concerning possessions as, "*they that buy*, (should live) *as though they possessed not.*"

11. What does this mean, and is it realistically possible to attain such a mind-set?

All people are also only for time, actually quite a short time. "For what is your life? It is even a vapour, that appeareth for a little time, and then vanisheth away" (James 4:14). And then in Hebrews 9:27, we see that after this short earthly life, man has an appointment to keep: "It is appointed unto men once to die, but after this the judgment."

12. Since this is the case with man and his things, how can we best "redeem the time," and be good stewards?
13. On what scripture or facts do you base your conclusion?
14. How can we protect ourselves against disappointment or regret about how we spent our days, when our time comes to leave this earth?

Everything belongs to God; we are only stewards for a time. "The earth is the Lord's and the fullness thereof" (Ps. 24:1). This is an all-inclusive assertion.

21. To what degree then, or in what way is it acceptable to say this is mine, I bought it; or, we own this or that?

Another important mind-set to have is that you are not the only person to be considered. "Look not every man on his own things, but every man also on the things of others" (Phil. 2:4). This has to do with living circumspectly as we read in Ephesians 5:15. Look around you; be considerate of other people and their circumstances and desires.

Unfortunately there are people who go charging through life, conscious only of their own goals and desires, likes and dislikes. This could be called living "tunnel-spectly," instead of circumspectly, seeing only your own little field of concerns. This makes people inconsiderate and selfish, brushing everyone else out of their way as they pursue what they think is for them.

22. This is not a healthy outlook. How can it be corrected?
23. Should everybody have a desire for better vision and understanding in this subject?

COMPLIANCE TO GOD'S ULTIMATE CONTROL

How much or how little we have or don't have doesn't matter a whole lot in the long run. God can multiply as He sees fit. Consider these examples.

First Chronicles 21:3, in Joab's reproof and encouragement to David: "The Lord make his people an hundred times so many more as they be: but, my lord the king, are they not all my lord's servants? why then doth my lord require this thing? why will he be a cause of trespass to Israel?"

Joshua 23:10: If they would be faithful, "one man of you shall chase a thousand."

First Kings 17:12-16, concerning the widow's meal and oil: "The barrel of meal shall not waste, neither shall the cruse of oil fail, until the day *that* the Lord sendeth rain upon the earth."

John 6:9-13: Five loaves and two fish, to feed 5000 men! And twelve baskets of leftovers besides?

Second Peter 3:8: "But, beloved, be not ignorant of this one thing, that one day is with the Lord as a thousand years, and a thousand years as one day."

1. Can the same be said for dollars, or other things?
2. How can we grasp and practice trust in God's promise of provision? See Matthew 6:33.

God can also diminish funds and substance or withhold increase as He sees fit.
Consider Haggai 1:5-11, about sowing much and reaping little, having clothes but not being warm, earning money put in bags (or purses) with holes in them, etc.

3. Why was it not going well; what was the problem?
4. Proverbs 23:5-b says, "For *riches* certainly make themselves wings; they fly away as an eagle toward heaven." Can you give an example of this?
5. If God can cause unexplainable increase or decrease beyond our control, at His will, to what degree are we yet required to put forth our best efforts?

According to biblical prophecies and world history, it is not reasonable to expect perpetual material and economic prosperity, even though it might seem normal. Remember the seven-year famine in Genesis chapter 41, the Great Depression in the United States and simultaneous drought of the1930s. And remember Job's experience: "The Lord gave, and the Lord has taken away" (Job 1:21). Job said, "shall we receive only good and not evil?" (Job 2:10).

6. What would you answer Job?
7. How can we stay prepared for economic downturns without "missing the boat" or being a doomsayer?

Tough times usually make us grow and prepare us for challenges ahead. Tough times made the Israelites willing to move out the land of

Goshen in Egypt, where they had formerly been enjoying very good circumstances.

8. Should we think of all tough times as "the making of us" for some future assignments or circumstances?
9. Should parents use this strategy to prepare their children for life as it really is?

Luke 16:8 says, "The children of this world are wiser than the children of light." In many cases that seems to be true about making profitable material and financial decisions and moves. Because they continually study these things, they may often be aware of money opportunities that Christian people won't be readily aware of, nor even interested in.

10. So: are Christians materially or financially disadvantaged because of their faith?
11. How does the second thought in Matthew 10:16 apply to this subject?

On the other hand, the teachings of the Bible, if followed, will make the Christian wiser than those who are on the wrong way. "Thou through thy commandments hast made me wiser than mine enemies (or those who do not obey God)" (Ps. 119:98). Psalm 19:7 says, "The law of the Lord is perfect, converting the soul: the testimony of the Lord is sure, making wise the simple."

12. Who then is a faithful and wise servant? (Matt. 24:45)
13. Is this kind of wisdom available to anyone?
14. To what extent is it correct for people, as they get more experience, to feel increasing confidence in their judgments and decisions?
15. In what ways does Bible knowledge shelter Christians from economic pitfalls or downturns and snares of erroneous lifestyles?

We often use the term *common sense*. (You can share your perception of what common sense is.) Isaiah, chapter 28, has a possible scriptural explanation of common sense. Starting in verse 23, it says there that a farmer will, or should, know when to plow and how to plant. We might say that he knows these things because of experience. That may well be so, but verse 26 says that "his God doth instruct him to discretion, and doth teach him." This would be the ultimate common sense, discretion from within that comes from God.

16. Is there anything we can personally do to acquire more common sense?
17. Do all people, whether they acknowledge God or not, have a measure of common sense?

Christians should hold "rather loosely" to the things of this earth. It should be that the stronger one's interest is in the things of God, the looser will be the grip on the things of this life. The Apostle Paul said that "all things are lawful unto me, but all things are not expedient: all things are lawful for me, but I will not be brought under the power of any" (1 Cor. 6:12).

18. What does it take to have the determination that Paul had?

A right attitude about money and possessions will have a positive effect in many, perhaps most, areas of life and will go a long way toward correcting many of life's problems. Your attitude about these things, right or wrong, says a lot about you.

19. Do you understand your own attitude about money and related things?
20. Is a right attitude well within everyone's reach?
21. Is it the same for all people and all eras?
22. Is the Bible the only source and the final authority on which to base our attitudes and goals concerning possessions and finances?

There is an interesting dialogue concerning our attitude and approach to life in Psalm 24:3-5. First is a question: "Who shall ascend into the hill of the Lord, or who shall stand in his holy place"?

Then the answer follows. "He that hath clean hands, and a pure heart; who hath not lifted up his soul unto vanity, nor sworn deceitfully. He shall receive the blessing from the Lord, and righteousness from the

God of his salvation." Take special notice of the term *clean hands*. This could cover a large scope.

23. How would you describe clean hands?
24. And a pure heart?

It has been said, "You may touch almost any area of people's lives, except their children and their wallet." It is true, these are two very sensitive areas of life, but surely Christians should not be untouchable. On the other hand, it is also possible to talk too freely and dispense undue information about your family, your things and circumstances, and create another set of problems.

25. What then, is a proper attitude toward these two subjects, and how openly should we talk about them?
26. How does Matthew 7:3-5 apply to this subject?

When it comes to being concerned about others around us, one must be careful because it is easy to take on a hawk-eyes attitude, or to inquire too freely or too much and become guilty of being a busybody in other men's matters.

27. What should one do if they think this is what someone else is doing to them?

In an effort to maintain a right state of mind and find direction to live by, remember Proverbs 3:5-6: "Trust in the Lord with all thine heart; and lean not unto thine own understanding. In all thy ways acknowledge him, and he shall direct thy paths."

Ponder the message of song #388 in the *Christian Hymnal*: "So let our lives and lips express, the Holy Gospel we profess . . ." (Isaac Watts).

Here is an interesting piece of poetry relevant to the right frame of mind about earthly things.

HOW DO YOU LIVE YOUR DASH?

I read of a man who stood to speak, at the funeral of a friend,
He referred to the dates on her tombstone, from the beginning... to the end.

He noted that first came her date of birth, and spoke of the following date with tears,
But he said what mattered most, was the dash between those years.
(1934–1998)

For that dash represents all the time, that she spent alive on earth,
And now only those who loved her, know what that little line is worth.

For it matters not how much we own; the cars, the house, the cash,
What matters is how we live and love, and how we spend our dash.

So think about this long and hard, are there things you'd like to change?
For you never know how much time is left, that can still be rearranged.

If we could just slow down enough, to consider what's true and real,
And always try to understand, what other people feel.

And be less quick to anger, and show appreciation more,
And love the people in our lives, like we've never loved before.

If we treat each other with respect, and more often wear a smile,
Remembering that this special little dash, might only last a little while.

So, when your eulogy's being read, with your life's actions to rehash,
Would you be proud of the things they say, about how you spent your dash?

—Author Unknown

The Christian Witness by Lifestyle and Business Manners

CHAPTER 2

Most people don't care where you go to church, what you say your preacher teaches, nor what you personally profess to believe, but they usually pass judgment about you, by what you are, the attitude you display, how you talk, and what you do.

What you do makes more noise than what you say. First Peter 2:12 says that you should have "your conversation (*way of life*), honest among the Gentiles: that, whereas they speak against you as evildoers, they may by your good works, which they shall behold, glorify God in the day of visitation."

1. How concerned should a person be about the foregoing facts?

Philippians 2:14-15 instructs us not to complain so that we will shine as lights in the world.

2. Does all complaining detract from the effectiveness of a Christian witness?
3. Is all complaining wrong?
4. How can a habitual complainer be helped?

Proverbs 4:18 says, "But the path of the just is (*or should be*), like the shining sun, that shines ever brighter unto the perfect day." This path refers to the way of life.

5. Can you explain the *shining* effect?
6. Does the term *ever brighter* mean that we will get better as we get older?

Honest and upright lifestyle and business ethics, may be our greatest impact of Christian influence and testimony to those around us. If we claim to be followers of Jesus, but our business dealings are not consistent with the Bible, we become hypocrites in the eyes of the observers. On the other hand, a humble life of integrity will speak volumes without saying a word. "You can preach a better sermon with your life than with your lips" (Oliver Goldsmith (1730 -1774). And again: "Preach the gospel everywhere. Use words if and when necessary" (from a sign by a church house).

A person's lifestyle, the way they do business, the way they relate to others, the issues they talk about, and their attitudes about general circumstances, say much about the person.

7. Is it possible to be a credible Christian witness without overall integrity?
8. How much should we be aware of what our life and conduct is saying to others?
9. How constantly conscious should one be of wanting to be a light to the world?
10. Is the quote by Oliver Goldsmith a scriptural philosophy?
11. If so, does it mean that one can relax and stay quiet?

Money matters can be a tough test of your character, especially when there is profit to be had by staying quiet or stating things just a bit different than they are. Christians should always "tell the truth, the whole truth, and nothing but the truth." Don't even shade it. Shaded things are hidden from full light, often allowing for some deception.

12. By truth and honesty, are you salting the earth?
13. Is your life a shining light to the world? (Matt. 5:13-16).
14. "How Reads Your Life-Book?" (Song #442, *Christian Hymnal*, by Charles W. Naylor)

Consider Hebrews 11:13-14. Those that say such things, (that they are pilgrims and strangers), declare plainly that they are in search of a heavenly country. General lifestyle such as elaborate housing and furnishings, fashionable attire, many possessions, and other earthly things can dim or invalidate one's testimony and witness as a Christian.

15. What kind of a lifestyle will present-day pilgrims and strangers have?
16. Will they be intently concerned about things?
17. Will everything in the house have to match and be without a scratch, etc.?
18. If you think the last sentence of the preceding paragraph is true, how does it work?

Potiphar trusted Joseph completely and "saw that the Lord was with him and that the Lord made all that he did to prosper in his hand" (Gen. 39:1-6). Potiphar's full trust was due to at least two facts: He realized the Lord's effect in Joseph's endeavors, and he saw Joseph's impeccable integrity.

19. How can a young man or lady gain that kind of reputation and respect today?

First Thessalonians 5:8 talks about being "children of the day." Christians who live a life of honesty and integrity are "of the day," and have nothing to hide or to be ashamed of.

20. What should one do if he realizes he has stepped "into the night" with a business deal?

"A good name is rather to be chosen than great riches, and loving favour rather than silver and gold" (Prov. 22:1). This speaks about doing business deals in all honesty and uprightness even if, as a result, it becomes necessary to forfeit profits or causes a financial setback. And perhaps someone may even consider you foolish or silly for endeavoring to abide by total honesty.

21. Are you "for sale"? What would it take to buy your integrity?
22. Could you be bought into a wrong or questionable deal with enough money?
23. What does it take to stand firm and true under the pressure of large and tantalizing, but unfair or dishonest gain?

"Dead flies cause the ointment of the apothecary to send forth a stinking savour: so doth a little folly him that is in reputation for wisdom and honour" (Ecc. 10:1). One little act of folly or cheating can quickly ruin one's good reputation and the validity of his testimony.

24. Why is it so easy to spoil one's good name, but so difficult to rebuild a broken, formerly good reputation?

First Thessalonians 4:11-12 instructs us to live a quiet life, do our own business, stay busy and walk honestly toward them that are without. First Peter 2:12-15 says, "Having your conversation honest among the Gentiles: that, whereas they speak against you as evildoers, they may by your good works, which they shall behold, glorify God in the day of visitation. Submit yourselves to every ordinance of man for the Lord's sake: whether it be to the king, as supreme; Or unto governors, as unto them that are sent by him for the punishment of evildoers, and for the praise of them that do well. For so is the will of God, that with well doing ye may put to silence the ignorance of foolish men."

25. How do we achieve the grace of letting our way of life cause others to glorify God and not us?
26. Is it commanded, or even possible, never to listen for the praise of men if one is living right and doing well?

At times the sincere Christian will be thought strange because of his values and practices. For example, perhaps some people won't understand why you have no life insurance, no retirement savings account, why you don't take interest, or why you are not "running to the max," or other beliefs you are endeavoring to live by. This becomes an issue of financial non-conformity to the world. When questions arise about this, we should, according to 1 Peter 3:15, always be ready and willing to give an answer to any questions about our faith and hope of the future, and our sense of direction for our life on the earth.

27. Can anyone learn how to do this in a free and unpretentious way?
28. Should everyone be willing to try, regardless of temperament or character type?
29. Is it easily possible to go overboard and have too much to say?

Sometimes onlookers, seeing actual or perceived faults, will say about a person who claims to be a Christian, "Well, if that person is a Christian, I don't want to be one." Hebrews 12:13-14 instructs us not to offend observers by making a misstep and leaving a distorted influence: "And make straight paths for your feet, lest that which is lame be turned out of the way; but let it rather be healed. Follow peace with all men, and holiness, without which no man shall see the Lord."

30. What responsibility do Christians have when they realize they have failed and offended an onlooker?
31. Is anyone ever justified in turning aside or becoming discouraged because of the faults of others?

The way you live and what you do, will help make the church and the Christian witness what it is and what it will be in the future. When your words and your actions say the same thing, the right thing, you will be a winner for the Lord! You can make a difference, one instance at a time. Every life will affect others, one generation after the next, for better or for worse. Be a positive influence.

32. Is everyone, without exception, a responsible participant?
33. What should you tell a person who thinks their influence is so insignificant that it doesn't count?

Stay focused on the good goal; ponder Proverbs 4:25-27: "Let thine eyes look right on, and let thine eyelids look straight before thee. Ponder the path of thy feet, and let all thy ways be established. Turn not to the right hand nor to the left: remove thy foot from evil."

YOU'RE WRITING A "GOSPEL," A CHAPTER EACH DAY,
BY THE DEEDS THAT YOU DO, BY THE WORDS THAT YOU SAY,
MEN READ WHAT YOU WRITE, WHETHER FAITHLESS OR TRUE,
SAY, WHAT IS THE "GOSPEL," ACCORDING TO YOU?

--GILBERT

Starting Out Right

CHAPTER 3

Parents should have a definite goal to teach their children to start out *on the right foot.* Children who are well taught to be faithful with their money and things will have a lifelong advantage for living a Christian life. They also will normally be better spouses and parents. They will be a positive influence wherever they live.

A good foundation usually does not happen by accident or without effort. Actual dollars-and-cents training is very much in order; however, teaching why and how basic principles apply will equip your child better for the unknown future than a knowledge of many details and formulas. Even if they did not receive proper teaching, children, youth and newly married couples are still responsible before God. They still can, and must develop their own convictions and understanding of how to start out on a good foundation.

1. How positive should parents feel that they are on the right course of training?
2. What can or should parents do if, after their children are grown, they see they have failed to impart proper example and teaching?
3. Are there any key things young people should do if their parents failed them?

Preparing children to start out right is much like passing the baton in a relay race. It must be done with deliberate care, not in great haste, or you will drop it in the passing. An understanding of God's laws and Bible principles must be passed from one generation to the next. Sometimes one generation hands the baton of direction for life too carelessly to the next runners in life, and sometimes the next runners are in such a great hurry that they fail to get a good hold of the baton before they are off and running. Consequently they drop it, and its value is then generally lost.

4. How can parents be helped to more carefully pass the baton of Bible principles?
5. How can youth be slowed down enough to get a good grasp on it before they run?

Parents need to bear in mind what it says in Proverbs 22:15: "Foolishness is bound in the heart of a child; but the rod of correction shall drive it far from him." This is an important step in helping their children start out right in life.

6. Can you give an explanation of Proverbs 22:15 in practical action?

Another important beginner's quality is to learn to "fear God," because "the fear of the Lord is the beginning of wisdom" (Prov. 9:10).

7. How does this fear of God begin to make one wise?

As much as possible, start every day in a meaningful way. Discipline yourself and your family to a structured devotional time. This will have a big, long term bearing on how you and your family will respond to the circumstances and happenings in your life. It will also have a positive effect in the many necessary decisions in life.

You may think that a daily slot of time devoted for Bible reading and prayer (devotions) is not worth very much, but if you stick to it, you will sooner or later reap the advantages of Proverbs 2:10-12: "When wisdom entereth into thine heart, and knowledge is pleasant unto thy soul; Discretion shall preserve thee, understanding shall keep thee: To deliver thee from the way of the evil man, from the man that speaketh froward things."

The Psalmist proclaimed, "My voice shalt thou hear *in the morning*, O Lord; *in the morning* will I direct my prayer unto thee, and will look up" (Ps. 5:3).

"Cause me to hear thy loving-kindness *in the morning;* for in thee do I trust: cause me to know the way wherein I should walk; for I lift up my soul unto thee" (Ps. 143:8).

8. Is morning a better time for family or personal devotion time than midday or evening?
9. If so, what shall parents do if the father has to leave for work before the children arise?
10. Is a once-a-week family devotion time worthwhile, or would you just as well skip the idea altogether?

Reading is a good way to learn many things and to gain wisdom. But choose your reading (and your listening) wisely because enduring exposure to any subject, whether positive or negative, will eventually hit home.

11. Do people actually become what they feed on mentally? See 1 Corinthians 15:33.
12. Does this also include trade magazines, etc.?

Learn to accept no for an answer and to master the fortitude to successfully tell yourself, no. Sometimes you will have to accept yes when you would prefer a no. If you don't understand, find someone to help you learn this necessary self-discipline.

13. Is it a never-ending challenge to keep one's wants or resistance under control?

Be willing to be instructed. "Whoso loveth instruction loveth knowledge: but he that hateth reproof *is* brutish" (Prov. 12:1). This applies to listening as well as reading.

An anonymous quote about the part of reading follows: "Education is what you get when you read the fine print. Experience is what you get when you don't." (Anonymous).

14. What is the necessary mind-set for desiring to be taught, or loving instruction?
15. An oft-repeated old adage says, "When all else fails, read the in-

structions." Will people always tend to be that way, skipping the instructions until the last resort?

The prodigal son (*wasteful, reckless, extravagant and uncontrolled*) in Luke 15:11-13 is certainly not an example of starting out right. He was in the wrong first by demanding what he considered was his share of the family assets. He was wrong a second time in what he did with it.

16. Which wrong was the biggest mistake?
17. Do people today still learn from the prodigal son's mistakes?

You need to have your earning ability functioning before you start spending. "Prepare thy work without, and make it fit for thyself in the field; and afterwards build thine house" (Prov. 24:27). This pertains to the fact that sustenance comes from the field, not from the house.

18. How much must a young man prove himself "in the field" before he is prepared to buy or to build a house?
19. How does this verse integrate with the teaching about taking "no thought for your life" (Luke 12:22-30)?

Another important issue for starting out right is for young people to learn maturity and to be responsible for themselves. How soon and how well this will be accomplished depends a lot on the parents, but also on the young people themselves. In Old Testament Israel, a young man was considered mature at age thirty. Many things may be different today, but the need of maturity remains the same.

20. What might be the meaning of the term, "he is of age," in John 9:21?
21. At what age do you think young people should be "on their own," controlling their own money and time and making their own decisions?
22. On what do you base your thinking?
23. The term "it is corban" in Mark 7: 9-13 was a means for children to justify not doing anything for their parents. Is that idea still causing problems today?
24. Is it a mistake when parents do not ask their minor children to give any of their earnings home?

25. Is it okay for parents to allow their adult children to live at home and pay nothing for room and board?

We find some thought about this subject in 1 Timothy 5:4: "Let them learn first to show piety at home, and *to requite their parents:* for that is good and acceptable before God." Even though this scripture is primarily teaching about the care of widows, it surely applies to children's general responsibility to their parents and other family members.

26. What do you think is meant by requiting their parents? And for what?

Allowing children to have their own money and freedom at a young age generally does not bring good results. There must be a reason why the age of 21 was for a long time considered as the right time to be "on your own." Parents; you really should have a plan of action in effect and understood, before your children grow up. There is more than one right way, but do have a goal. It is a good idea to properly record your plan in writing, for the good of the parents and the children. Trying to decide or organize such things in a crisis is not good. If you haven't done it yet, it would be a wise idea to do it now.

The blessing promised to children in Ephesians 6:1-3 applies to this subject. Children who cheerfully submit to their parent's plan will surely be blessed for it in the long run.

27. Would a more uniform practice among families in a church community help to avoid stress and problems between parents and children in this area?
28. How much should parents concern themselves about how others are doing it?
29. What can parents do if their children think what is required of them is not fair?
30. How is it that many who don't have access to much money when they are quite young will in a few years often be ahead of those who did?

To achieve a reasonable success parents need to invest considerable time and effort, teaching and showing their children how to do things, and then require obedience and hold them accountable for their actions. Real life will require that of them.

31. What are some good ways to help children learn how to make decisions and how to use their money skillfully?
32. Must parents always explain their reasons for doing, or not doing, things? Won't children just catch on?
33. How does one hold children accountable for their actions?

A lot of easy money does not promote responsibility or a proper sense of value; in fact, it is often a definite hindrance. Idle hours and easy dollars are not a good recipe for the youth years (usually not for older folks either).

34. What can or should be done about this?

Christian young people need much more than lots of money to be prepared for marriage. They need a good knowledge of God's rules and a willing and practical knowledge of how to work. Work is after all the answer for most of life's needs.

35. Can parents know when they have given their children enough training to face life on their own?
36. What can parents go by to help them decide if their children have sufficient financial means for marriage?
37. By what can young people best gauge their own perceptions in this issue?

Young people, what you do with your first earnings can affect your finances for the rest of your life. Ecclesiastes 11:9-10 says, "Rejoice, O young man, in thy youth; and let thy heart cheer thee in the days of thy youth, and walk in the ways of thine heart, and in the sight of thine eyes: *but know thou, that for all these things God will bring thee into judgment.* Therefore remove sorrow from thy heart, and put away evil from thy flesh: for childhood and youth are vanity."

Young people will gain a lifetime of advantage if they invest their first earnings in necessary and honorable things, instead of on unneeded or overly costly clothing and vehicles, or unnecessary and even frivolous things.

A certain man of the past, when he was a teenager, would go out at night and catch barn pigeons in his father's and neighbors' barns. These he sold to earn some money for himself. When he died at ninety-some years old, it was said figuratively, that he still had his pigeon money. He was thereby given the credit that he had not foolishly or wastefully spent his monies. Far too many young people spend their "pigeon money" already before they get married and start out on their own.

38. Does every young man who squanders his early earnings suffer at least some negative consequences?
39. If so, do these negative consequences sometimes follow a person all the way through life?
40. Does this apply equally to young ladies?
41. How would you explain Ecclesiastes 11:10, about childhood and youth being vanity?

It has been said that a man has two chances to get financially established in life. The first opportunity is before he gets married and the second is when his family is old enough to help earn the family's livelihood.

42. If you think this is true, explain your perception of why and how.

The money you do not spend in your youth can have many positive effects, all the way to the end of your days on the earth.

43. Share some ideas why and how this works.
44. Could it be possible that the effects will even reach into eternity?

Whether or not it's easy or hard to get started in life depends on you and what you think you need. It is always wise to start out well within your means. Normally it's hard or impossible to start off in high gear, at a high level of living. If you want things to function properly, you must learn to live within *your* means and *your* abilities.

45. How should young people calculate their means?
46. Does it make any difference whether one is quite young, or already a bit older?

47. Can a humble, honest person readily discern the limits of his abilities?
48. Are make-or-break ventures ever in order for Christians?

"Where no counsel is, the people fall: but in the multitude of counsellors there is safety" (Prov. 11:14). There is much value in asking for advice and opinion from other people, especially those who have experience with the issue in question.

There are many stories and testimonies of people who rose from seemingly hopeless circumstances as they sought and followed the counsel of other people. There is also value in soliciting opinions from a variety of others, some of who, though inexperienced, may be just as able to share unbiased observations and recommendations as those directly involved in the issue.

49. When you ask for counsel from a number of people, they will usually not all give the same advice. Should one ask many people anyway?
50. What should one do if the direction of the advisors is totally scattered?
51. What should you do if the advice is unified, but you don't like it?
52. When the counsel is all the same, is it always right to follow it?

There is an old and often told story about seeking and utilizing advice. A farmer, not too well educated, went to town and saw a sign which said, "Advice, two dollars." Since he did not know what advice was, he decided to buy some and find out. When he asked to purchase some advice, he was asked what kind of advice he wanted. Still not understanding, he said, "Whatever you have for me. I just thought I would buy some and take it along home."

Seizing the opportunity, the man told the farmer to wait a bit and he would be right back with some advice for him. When he returned, he handed the man an envelope, told him not to open it until he was home, and charged him the two dollars.

When the farmer got home he found nothing but a piece of paper in the envelope. On the paper it said, "Never put off until tomorrow what you can do today." At first the farmer became angry, thinking he had been cheated. After a bit though, he thought that perhaps he should do what the paper said and bring in some hay that was ready to be brought into the barn.

The following day turned out to be a rainy day, and the man was very grateful that his hay was safely stored in his dry barn. Contemplating a bit, he concluded that the two dollars was well spent. Now he understood the meaning of advice.

53. Do even well educated people sometimes have a problem understanding what advice is and how to utilize it?

When it's time to make decisions concerning earthly matters, your attitude, reasons and motives often mean more than the exact details of a matter.

Let your plans and goals be subject to God's will, according to the teaching in James 4:13-17: "Go to now, ye that say, Today or tomorrow we will go into such a city, and continue there a year, and buy and sell, and get gain: Whereas ye know not what shall be on the morrow. For what is your life? It is even a vapour, that appeareth for a little time, and then vanisheth away. For that ye ought to say, If the Lord will, we shall live, and do this, or that. But now ye rejoice in your boastings: all such rejoicing is evil. Therefore to him that knoweth to do good, and doeth it not, to him it is sin."

54. Should we *always* say, "If The Lord will . . ."?
55. What else can we learn from this scripture?

Young people, as well as all others, you will do well to think more about becoming a person of value, than being obsessed with becoming a great success story.

56. What will make one the "person of value" one should strive to become?
57. Do the same things apply to boys and girls?

Live by the Golden Rule (Matt. 7:12) and all other Bible principles; they work! God can however, make exceptions at His will. An honest endeavor to follow the Bible opens the way for God to bless your life with good things as He sees fit.

58. Can these blessings reach beyond your own life to the life of others?
59. Does God bless even unbelievers who follow basic Bible principles?

Around 1835 a Frenchman named Alexis de Tocqueville spent several years studying U.S. democracy and economy. In a book about his findings, he wrote the following thought. "It was not until I went into America's churches, and heard the sermons flaming from the pulpits that I understood that America is great, because America is good. And if ever America ceases to be good, America will cease to be great."

60. If we cease to live by the rules of the Bible, will the blessings cease to flow?
61. If yes, why? Isn't God long suffering?

Whatever your challenges are, whatever the problems you face, or whatever your quest in life, the best place to start on improvement or correction is right where you are.

62. Is it true that no matter where a person is, when they want to start doing what is right, they are standing at the beginning of the right road?

THINGS WORK OUT BEST FOR THOSE
WHO MAKE THE BEST OF THE WAY THINGS WORK OUT.
By Art Linkletter from "Bits and Pieces"

Family Involvements and Interactions

CHAPTER 4

Psalm 127:3 declares, "Lo, children are an heritage of the Lord: and the fruit of the womb is his reward." First Timothy 5:14, referring to potential problems, says, "I will therefore that the younger women marry, bear children, guide the house, give none occasion to the adversary to speak reproachfully."

1. Are these verses still true and applicable?

Because of the time and circumstances of today, and because of choices made possible by modern medical technology, young couples need to beware of an anti-children mentality. Sometimes the thought arises that because of how things are in the world, it would be better not to bring children into the world. Sometimes young couples experience an honest fear about having children.

There is also a potential of subtle, erroneous thinking about having a family and feeling that children would be a hindrance to fulfillment in life. Children are in fact a hindrance to those in pursuit of selfish pleasures, but for those who are serious about serving the Lord, it is normally a blessing to have and to care for a family.

Luke 23:29 speaks about some who would pronounce a blessing on those who never had any children. It is not talking about those in God's service but about some who are not ready to meet the Lord.

2. If a couple has no desire for a family, is there always something wrong?
3. When a mother finds mothering a drag with little or no joy, what is the problem?

On the other hand there are couples who are unable to have a family. This is not only a modern-day problem. There are numerous illustrations in the Bible about people who dealt with this issue.

4. Are there scriptures that relate to family choices made possible by modern-day medical technology? If so, what are they?
5. When a couple realizes that this appears to be their lot in life, is it acceptable to pull out all stops, financially and otherwise, in an effort to attain their desire for children, biological or adopted?

Those who do have a family sometimes tend to become overly concerned about how they will pay all the costs of feeding and clothing their family, and the many other expenditures that are connected to raising a family. Can parents still afford to have a family today? In the past, and even today in other nations, people have raised, and are raising families in economic conditions far below the good circumstances in present-day North America.

Jesus taught about this very subject in Matthew 6:25-34, basically telling the people, Don't worry; don't question, What shall we eat, or What will we wear?

God has promised to provide for the daily needs: "Consider the lilies how they grow: they toil not, they spin not; and yet I say unto you, that Solomon in all his glory was not arrayed like one of these. If then God so clothes the grass, which is to day in the field, and tomorrow is cast into the oven; how much more will he clothe you, O ye of little faith? And seek not ye what ye shall eat, or what ye shall drink, neither be ye of doubtful mind. For all these things do the nations of the world seek after: and your Father knoweth that ye have need of these things" (Luke 12:27-30).

One grandmother encouraged younger couples not to worry, because with every baby God sends another living. This statement carries a lot of truth and should bring comfort.

6. What does *of a doubtful mind* mean?
7. Is not to worry about these things a matter of choice?
8. Can proper planning and mind-discipline lessen the tendency to worry?
9. How much worry is brought on by trying to live too high or too complicated a lifestyle?

For the family in progress, a soundly structured, well-disciplined home and family life has tremendous value to both the parents and the children, now and in the future. Practicing these virtues will add profound merit and meaning to your home and family life. An established and consistent order provides a calmness and sense of security for the whole family. These things have much to do with the spiritual and social success of your home life, for you and your family. It relates closely to emotional and physical well being. And believe it or not, it also ultimately relates closely to successful family finances.

Good, solid home structure and successful homes do not happen by chance. It requires vision, at least some planning, and diligent discipline. Predictable daily routine may at times seem tedious, but it is very valuable in the long run. It has much to do with learning self-discipline and productivity in life.

Following are a few points of structure to consider:

- Consistent and appropriate rising time in the morning
- Scheduled spiritual devotion time for the family
- Planned and routine meal times
- Scheduled chore assignments and times
- Designated and well-defined responsibilities
- Planned and adequate departure times for church, school, work, and other regular activities
- Customary and disciplined bed times
- Scheduled or routine service and maintenance of your house and appliances, etc
- Any necessary things appropriate for your family and circumstances

10. What would you add to the list?
11. Would you delete anything?
12. Can you share an experience about solid home structure from your own childhood or from your experience as a parent that might encourage others?
13. Can you quote any scriptures that relate to the subject?

Ephesians 6:1-3 has some teachings that appeal directly to the children. It implies that children can buy themselves a long-life blessing.

Children, you can purchase this blessing if you "honor your father and your mother (your family and household policies)." "It's a promise. Turn to the scripture and check it out. And remember, even Jesus "was subject to his parents" (Luke 2:51).

14. What are some ways for parents to "hold out a carrot stick" to motivate their children to follow family and household policies?

Ephesians 6:1-3 explains God's preferred relationship of children to their parents. But, fathers *(and mothers)*, you have a big assignment to be devout leaders in your home and to actually be honor worthy. Proverbs 31:11-28 gives the recipe for mothers *(and fathers)* to live by so their children will call them "blessed." Many other Scriptures relate to godly parenting.

According to Proverbs 22:6, if you do what you can to teach your children the right principles when they are young, years later you will most likely have the blessing of seeing them live by those teachings.

15. What quality or strength of character can parents acquire that will keep them from growing weary in well doing as a parent?

Many parents who are otherwise good teachers and disciplinarians fall short on training their children in financial discipline. Child training in natural things is just as important as spiritual things. A positive example is the most important tool whereby parents can teach and train their children the good way. This is most successfully accomplished by a long-term "show and tell" session. Careless and undisciplined parents rarely succeed in turning their children into responsible adults. Normally you cannot impart to your children what you don't live yourself. There is a real danger of becoming too busy with personal interests and being excessively occupied with the wrong things.

16. Is the first sentence of this paragraph true?
17. If so, why?
18. Is there anything parents of grown children can do if they see they have failed?

Proper honor, respect and down-to-earth communication are necessary, first of all between parents; and then between parents and children it is also immensely important. This helps to prepare children for marriage and for the financial responsibility of house and home management. Unfortunately it seems that respect in general is at low ebb in society, and therefore there is a great need for encouragement of this virtue in Christian families.

19. Must every couple learn their own way of showing respect and communicating?
20. What can be done to promote more healthy and respectful demeanor and daily comportment?

Proverbs 20:7 gives this thought that a godly father, who lives a life of integrity, is preparing the way for his children to be blessed after him. This fact is true in many ways. It applies spiritually and socially as well as financially.

One of a man's five sons went to his father's bank to borrow some money. "Yes," said the banker, "I will help you." When he started to fill in the loan application, the banker said, "Now let's see, which one of the boys are you?" He placed his confidence in this son, whose name he didn't even know, because the father's integrity had paved the way for him.

21. How much should parents be aware of this and specifically endeavor to pave the way of blessing for their children?
22. For about how many generations do the traits and advantages of a good home follow a family line?

Proverbs 15:27 addresses the other side of the issue: "He that is greedy of gain troubleth his own house; but he that hateth gifts shall live."

23. What kind of trouble does a greedy father bring on his family?
24. In the above verse, what's the issue about hating gifts?

Generally a newly married couple should pool their money and establish a joint checking account. It should no longer be his money and her money. For the health of the marriage it should now be our money and our things. Husbands must remember though, that they have not purchased their wife and they don't *own* her as a servant. Husbands, treat her with fairness and respect.

Under some circumstances separate accounts are in order. It can be beneficial and rewarding for the wife to have an account to manage household expenses. If they choose to do this, the husband must allocate sufficient funds. The wife on the other hand, must prove herself to be trustworthy and spend carefully and wisely.

If a couple is self-employed, as in farming or a business venture, it is almost compulsory to have a separate checking account for business income and expenses only. This greatly facilitates record keeping and should keep business funds from disappearing for personal wants.

25. Who is responsible to help young couples find their way in these things?

A wife's spirit and attitude can have lots to do with whether or not her husband is successful in life. If she is a loving, discreet and obedient keeper of the home, as in Titus 2: 4-5, she will be a strong, helpful influence. "She will do him good and not evil all the days of her life" (Prov. 31:12). A virtuous woman is a crown to her husband (Prov. 12:4). Blessed indeed is the husband whose wife is a willing, cheerful and contented homemaker for her husband and family. This is a vital part of their success in life.

26. Some people say, "The woman sets the mood of the home." Is that true?
27. What is the husband's part in this issue?

NECESSITY AND BLESSINGS OF MARRIAGE UNITY

Husbands and wives should be very open to each other and jointly knowledgeable of their financial circumstances and goals, as well as things like mortgage balances, location of legal documents and important papers, etc. Properly integrated couples should find it a satisfying joy to manage their finances as a team. For proper team living, wives need to show appropriate interest and share the concerns about how things are going for them and what their objectives are in life. If you have trouble communicating on this level, by all means get help!

28. Young couples should have the talent and ability of team living by the time they get married. How or from whom should they have learned this?
29. What should a wife do if she thinks her husband is too protective or secretive about their financial circumstances or legal arrangements?
30. Where should legal documents be stored?

It is important to communicate about finances. Many marriage counselors say that most of the time disagreements about money and related things are either at or very close to the top of problems in troubled marriages. Many Christian ministers say similar things. So, complete openness and freedom to discuss these issues in all charity and honesty and find answers together, will give you a better chance for a happy marriage.

31. If you are a young person, do you have any questions about this subject?
32. If you are advanced in years, do you have any counsel for young couples about this issue?

Another important reason for close cooperation is the fact that most married women will become widows and will have to face life without their husbands. It happens too often that a husband dies, and his wife is ill prepared to go on without him because she knows little about their affairs and where to find necessary information, etc. If the wife is uninterested, or the husband deliberately keeps his wife in the dark about their circumstances, the problem will be magnified.

33. Should couples regularly speak about this issue?
34. What should a wife do if she knows that her husband is deliberately keeping her in the dark about things?

In their efforts to establish this close teamwork, husbands need to be cautious not to expect too much of their wives. This can happen in numerous ways. Sometimes husbands don't understand how much work it is to run the house. It can happen that a husband does not like bookwork and record keeping, or he thinks he is too busy, and he dumps the responsibility on his wife. Sometimes husbands forget to "give honor unto the wife, as unto the weaker vessel" (1 Pet. 3:7).

35. Does every couple need to find their own balance in how to be teammates?
36. What should a wife do if she feels forced to take charge of finances or other things because her husband seems to be unconcerned or unwilling to take his responsibility?

Sometimes the wife has a quicker or better financial comprehension and balance than the husband does. This does not need to spell trouble for them. Such a wife has a challenge to know how to be her husband's helper, without criticizing him or running ahead of him. By pulling together they can be a successful team.

37. Are there some tips for the husband whose wife appears to surpass him in understanding financial issues?
38. What will keep the husband from feeling inferior?
39. How would you describe the act of pulling together, regardless of either spouse's makeup?

INCLUDING YOUR CHILDREN

When children have grown beyond being babies, they should be included to some degree in knowledge of the family's finances and the criteria for making decisions so they can learn by exposure. This will normally give them a better financial foundation than having their own money to learn with.

It is usually true that "the family that prays (and works) together, stays together." This ideal way of team living generally does not happen by itself. It requires some foresight and planning by the parents, followed by participation from everyone to make it work.

Children can be taught not to tell everything they know about their parents' financial circumstances; however, even if your schoolteacher finds out what your mortgage balance is, normally nothing bad happens. So don't be overly secretive with your family.

1. What is required on the parents' part to be willing to allow their children to know the family's financial circumstances and other such things?

2. If this ideal is accomplished, will it automatically result in a strong family bond?

There will also be times when things will not go well for some families. Then parents must be careful not to make their children feel guilty or at fault for the failure. The parents are, after all, the ones who carry the responsibility. They must be careful not to vent their frustrations on their children, which could unjustly provoke the children to wrath or rebellion. Consider Ephesians 6:4.

It can be very beautiful though, if parents can help their children understand that things have not gone well, and everyone needs to sacrifice in order to find a way to a successful end.

3. Is this asking too much for parents when things have gone wrong?
4. Can onlookers help in such situations?

Children are the happiest when they are involved and occupied, especially learning "grown-up" things. Real-life involvements can teach better than words. Children who are allowed or even encouraged, in a supervised way, to stretch the limits of their abilities have an advantage that will follow them through life.

Children also have an advantage if they are taught the security of a controlled lifestyle in finances as well as other things. Well-taught and well-disciplined children always stand a good chance to become successful and honorable citizens, of use to their fellow man, and a glory to God.

5. How should parents respond if they suffer financial loss because they allowed their children to stretch the limits of their abilities too far?
6. Do you think children should be included in making decisions about when and what to buy for the family, or the business if they have one?

Home projects, such as gardening, raising poultry, or any educational projects that instill virtues and character values, are usually worth more than they cost, or more than the profit they might generate. If parents fail to look beyond the present, they may too easily conclude it is too much bother or financially unwise.

7. What are some of the values to be gained by such ventures?
8. Can you share an encouraging experience or memory about this subject?

To help them develop right attitudes, children should not be paid for every little job or chore they do at home. Those who are, tend to grow up thinking that the world owes them for everything they do, and likely they will not be willing givers. Children who grow up pampered and having everything handed to them, so to speak, are at a disadvantage in life. On the other hand, those who grow up exposed to some of the tough side of life tend to fare better in their adult life. It has something to do with being forced to improvise and to develop ingenuity and perseverance. This might be some of the meaning about sowing in tears and reaping in joy (Ps. 126:5).

The instructions for a small egg incubator had an interesting but serious point. It said that when you see that the chicks are starting to peck to break their way out of the egg, you must resist the temptation to take over and break open the egg to help the struggling chick out. If you do, the chick will likely die, because they need the hatching struggle to survive. There may be a lesson in this for parents concerning their children. If you never allow them to struggle, you will probably hinder them in the long run.

9. Should parents, then, sometimes deliberately make things tough for their children to give them a chance to learn any consequent virtues and values?
10. Should parents at times stand back and allow their children to struggle, or even to suffer a bit, for their betterment in the long run?
11. If so, is natural love sometimes a hindrance to this type of schooling?

In a proper family setting, young children don't need money. The virtuous woman (or the parents) feeds and clothes the family. See Proverbs 31:10-22. However, as the children grow older and begin to think they need money, let them earn some, but not *too much*. Earning their own money is one of the better ways for children to learn the value of money.

A father told about an occasion when his teenage son asked if he could have a certain item. The father said, "I have no objections to that."

The son responded, "Well, but I will need money to buy it."

"Of course," said the father, "get some."

"Oh," said the son, "but the other boys say their fathers just give them the money."

Then the father replied, "Well, that is them, this is you and me. If you want to buy one of those things, get yourself an after school job and earn the money and you can buy it."

Some years later, in answer to a question about the result of his teaching, this man attested to feeling well satisfied about how things turned out with his children. He said they are now well able to take care of themselves.

12. Should children ever be handed a regular free allowance from the family fund?
13. What are the usual results if parents love their children so much that they can't keep themselves from handing their children everything that would be nice to have?

The Scripture does not indicate that parents are responsible to set their children up with a plush start in life. A good example, a realistic education and outlook, practical experience and spiritual tools to work with are worth far more than any ready-made situation. This adage still applies today: "Give a man a fish and you have fed him for a day. Teach him how to fish, and you have fed him for his life."

14. Would it help parents to be more diligent in practical training if they were constantly conscious of what they hope to have accomplished for their children by the time they leave home?

All of these things will take time, effort, and sometimes a good bit of expense. The parents that become too intent on making money will probably reap negative effects. This is likely some of what it means in Proverbs 15:27: "He that is greedy of gain troubleth his own house."

In contrast, for those parents, or more precisely, those fathers who are willing to make any necessary sacrifices and who do not grow weary in well doing, Psalm 112:1-2 says, "Blessed is the man that feareth the Lord, that delighteth greatly in his commandments. His seed shall be mighty upon earth: the generation of the upright shall be blessed."

Abraham's household had the promise of a blessing from God: "For I know him, that he will command his children and his household after him, and they shall keep the way of the Lord, to do justice and judgment; that the Lord may bring upon Abraham that which he hath spoken of him" (Gen. 18:19).

This chapter is only a scratch on the surface of this vast subject of family involvements and interaction and its many implications.

15. Do you have input or questions about any points of the subject that are not addressed in this discourse?
16. Do you have any concluding thoughts to share about the family issues?

ONE PERSON EXEMPLIFYING PRACTICAL CHRISTIAN LIVING
IS WORTH MORE THAN MANY SERMONS.

Neighborhood Relationships and Conduct

CHAPTER 5

There are about 150 direct references in the KJV Bible about neighbors. There are many others that suggest neighborly "do's" and "don'ts."

Of prime importance are a few New Testament updates from the Old that command us to love our neighbors. Jesus called loving our neighbors the second commandment in Matthew 22:39: "And *the second* is like unto it, Thou shalt love thy neighbour as thyself." How is this possible? How are we going to do it?

James 2:8 uses similar wording: "If ye fulfill the royal law according to the scripture, Thou shalt love thy neighbour as thyself, ye do well." And Romans 13:10 has another thought along the same lines: "Love worketh no ill to his neighbour: therefore love is the fulfilling of the law." Along with other things, this scripture instructs us not to misuse or take advantage of a neighbor.

1. Is it possibly too idealistic to be able to love any and all neighbors like ourselves?
2. What do you think *working no ill to neighbors* means?

Honesty between neighbors is perhaps right next to love in importance for neighborly conduct. Several scriptures refer to this aspect of association with our neighbors.

"These are the things that ye shall do; Speak ye every man the truth to his neighbour; execute the judgment of truth and peace in your gates: And let none of you imagine evil in your hearts against his neighbour; and love no false oath: for all these are things that I hate, saith the Lord" (Zech. 8:16-17).

"Wherefore putting away lying, speak every man truth with his neighbour: for we are members one of another" (Eph. 4:25). It appears to be important that we shall be careful not to deceive or mislead our neighbor in any way.

3. What would cause the temptation to be untruthful with a neighbor?
4. To be truthful, must we always tell the neighbor *everything* about an issue?

Possibly number three in neighborly importance is to be peaceful. "If it be possible, as much as lieth in you, live peaceably with all men" (Rom. 12:18). "We then that are strong ought to bear the infirmities of the weak, and not to please ourselves. Let every one of us please his neighbour for his good to edification" (Rom. 15:1-2).

Do what you can to avoid conflict with your neighbors. Abraham left a good example in the stress between him and his nephew Lot (Gen. 13: 1-12). So did Isaac when there was strife with the Philistines over water wells (Gen. 26:12-22). Both of these righteous men peacefully conceded to others to avoid conflict.

If you encounter problems, go promptly but peacefully, humbly and cautiously, and talk them over. Proverbs 25:8-10 says, "Go not forth hastily to strive, lest thou know not what to do in the end thereof, when thy neighbour hath put thee to shame. Debate thy cause with thy neighbour himself; and discover not a secret to another: Lest he that heareth it put thee to shame, and thine infamy turn not away."

5. Do the examples of Abraham and Isaac still apply to today's conditions?
6. Do they still work?
7. What can be done if the neighbor seems determined to be confrontational or otherwise always disagreeable?
8. What does it mean to *debate your cause*?

Here's more about the issue of peace with a neighbor. There is a searching two-part question in Psalm 15:1: "*Lord, who shall abide in thy tabernacle? Who shall dwell in thy holy hill?*" Part of the answer is in verse three. "He that backbiteth not with his tongue, nor doeth evil to his neighbour, nor taketh up a reproach against his neighbour."

First Peter 4:15 says, "But let none of you suffer . . . as a busybody in other men's matters." This would surely include your neighbor's matters. This is important in neighborly associations. The admonition is, mind your own business and stay out of trouble. It relates to gossip, nose-poking, unsolicited or excessive opinion passing, or otherwise making a nuisance of yourself.

9. Should the new nature referred to in 2 Corinthians 5:17 automatically make us good neighbors and keep us from the faults listed above?

Those who qualify as our neighbors don't always live close to us; they might only happen to be close to us at a time of need. The account of the Good Samaritan in Luke 10:25-37 tells of such a neighbor. That certain Samaritan became known as the Good Samaritan because he showed mercy to a neighbor in need.

10. In the scripture reference above, how would you answer the lawyer's question, "And who is my neighbor?"

It's a good idea to stay in your neighbor's good will so you can go to him in trouble. Good neighbors are worth more than distant relatives in times of need. This is what it says in Proverbs 27:10; "Thine own friend, and thy father's friend, forsake not; neither go into thy brother's house in the day of thy calamity: *for better is a neighbour that is near than a brother far off.*"

11. Do you know any practical examples of Proverbs 27:10?
12. Considering today's communication technology, does this scripture still apply?

To be a pleasant neighbor, stop and think before you call or go over to their house. Proverbs 27:14 tells us, "He that blesseth his friend with a loud voice, rising early in the morning, it shall be counted a curse to him." This insinuates that though he is pronouncing a blessing on his neighbor, it might be offensive because it is too early (or too late) for the neighbor. Be discreet; don't be distasteful or offensive by being thoughtless or inconsiderate. Avoid calling too early or unreasonably late. With today's communication possibilities, time zones need to be considered before you make long distance or international phone calls.

13. What is proper conduct when someone calls or otherwise disturbs you too early or too late?
14. What should you do if you realize you did it to someone else?

When you go visiting, don't wear out your welcome. Don't go too often, or stay too long or too late when you visit. "Withdraw thy foot from thy neighbour's house; lest he be weary of thee, and so hate thee" (Prov. 25:17).

15. Are there any practical time guides to help avoid such problems?
16. Is this subject different for every culture?

Do good to your neighbor in need, if you can. "Withhold not good from them to whom it is due, when it is in the power of thine hand to do it. Say not unto thy neighbour, Go, and come again, and tomorrow I will give; when thou hast it by thee. Devise not evil against thy neighbour, seeing he dwelleth securely by thee" (Prov. 3:27-29).

17. What's this about telling your neighbor to go and come again tomorrow?
18. Can you share an example of Christians being a security for their neighbors?
19. Do Christians afford more security to their neighbors than non-Christian neighbors?

Another neighborly act of kindness is to rejoice with your neighbors when a good thing happens for them. "And when he cometh home, he calleth together his friends and neighbours, saying unto them, Rejoice with me" (Luke 15:6).

20. Should a person always be on the alert for opportunities to rejoice with their neighbors?
21. Does this require any special graces?

In addition to being a good neighbor to the public, Christians must particularly be able to get along well with others in the church. "As we have therefore opportunity, let us do good unto all men, especially unto them who are of the household of faith" (Gal. 6:10).

22. Why do some folks seem to get along fine with their neighbors but blend poorly with the household of faith?
23. Why does it say *especially*?

Be careful about comparing yourself, or competing with your neighbors, and perhaps feeling inferior or superior in yourself and your approach to life and work. The instructions from 2 Corinthians 10:12 apply to this issue: "For we dare not make ourselves of the number, or compare ourselves with some that commend themselves: but they measuring themselves by themselves, and comparing themselves among themselves, are not wise."

24. What should a person do if they see their neighbor doing things or owning things that appear to be better (or worse) than their own?
25. What happens when people spend too much time comparing or competing?

The following paragraphs have a few more specific do not's concerning neighbors:

Be wise; do not despise or denounce your neighbor. "He that is void of wisdom despiseth his neighbour: but a man of understanding holdeth his peace" (Prov. 11:12). In other words, if there actually is something negative about your neighbor, consider your own attitude and keep your mouth shut.

26. But shouldn't you warn the other neighbors about your proving?

Do not envy your neighbor. "I considered all travail, and every right work, that for this a man is envied of his neighbour. This is also vanity and vexation of spirit" (Ecc. 4:4). This seems to be speaking about keeping up with the Joneses. It is much better to concentrate on what is right for us as we endeavor to follow the Lord, than what Mr. Jones has or does.

27. Is it always wrong to look at what our successful neighbor has, or what he is doing?

Do not associate too freely or too carelessly with your neighbors, especially with those who do not honor the Lord. God warned the Israelites about this in Exodus 23:31-33: "And I will set thy bounds from the Red Sea even unto the Sea of the Philistines, and from the desert unto the river: for I will deliver the inhabitants of the land into your hand; and thou shalt drive them out before thee. Thou shalt make no covenant with them, nor with their gods. They shall not dwell in thy land, lest they make thee sin against me: for if thou serve their gods, it will surely be a snare unto thee."

The children of Israel failed in this matter. Psalm 106:35-36 says, "But they were mingled among the heathen, and learned their works. And they served their idols: which were a snare unto them."

To help us to stay on course in this issue, we need to remember what it says in 1 Corinthians 15:33; "Be not deceived: evil communications corrupt good manners."

28. Can you name some guidelines or safeguards concerning this issue?

Do not succumb to wrong communication with your neighbors. First Corinthians 15:33 says, "Be not deceived: evil communications corrupt good manners." This also relates to being too closely connected or too sociable with those who are not living Christian lives.

29. "Can two walk together, except they be agreed?" (Amos 3:3).

One more don't: do not conform. Being neighborly is good, but because of the human makeup and how people tend to follow each other, it becomes necessary for Christians to always be on guard against the negative influence of neighbors who are not following the Lord. Romans 12:2 tells us, "And be not conformed to this world: but be ye transformed by the renewing of your mind, that ye may prove what *is* that good, and acceptable, and perfect, will of God."

Now reconsider all the do's of being a good neighbor.

30. What are the most important qualities of neighborliness?

Responsibility, Accountability, Self-discipline and Diligence

CHAPTER 6

This is a weighty subject and therefore it is one of the longer chapters in this study. The title names key Christian virtues. Irresponsibility and lack of self-control cause many and huge problems for people. Slothfulness, the opposite of diligence, and unwillingness to be accountable for one's actions become a big hindrance if not a total roadblock to success in life. The lack of these virtues causes many social and financial stresses for a lot of individuals and often incites friction between individuals as well as many other problems.

1. An old adage says, "Easy come; easy go." Does it have to be so?
2. Does deeper Christian sincerity bring better self-control in the things of this life?
3. Is every person accountable to God for how they manage their earthly things?
4. What are some good ways for parents to instill accountability in their children?
5. From where does one get the ability to be diligent?

Consider Matthew 16:24-26, "If any man will come after me, let him deny himself, and take up his cross, and follow me. For whosoever will save his life shall lose it: and whosoever will lose his life for my sake shall find it. For what is a man profited, if he shall gain the whole world, and lose his own soul? or what shall a man give in exchange for his soul?"

Self-denial and discipline does not come naturally; it requires vision and a commitment to God's rules. Self-denial does not mean you can't have any of your personal desires; it is more akin to restraining the depraved nature and keeping things under control and in God's order, so you can enjoy His blessing.

Because of the imperfect human make-up, you will always need to keep saying no (to your depraved nature and desires) and actually put it into practice. One reason many people get hung up on this subject is that they may seem willing to do whatever it takes to correct a problem, as long as they can still have and do whatever they want. If your commitment is weak, and you don't learn and practice self-restraint, things will not go well.

There will also be times you will need to apply a definite "yes" mind-set, when you would much rather say no. This can test your resolve as much as the other way around.

The need for self-restraint applies in three basic ways:

- Spiritually and socially
- Mentally and physically
- Financially and in economic lifestyle decisions

6. What is the key mentality for mastering the word, *no*?
7. Can you give an example of needing to say yes when you would rather say no?
8. How can a person overcome *consuming desires* for whatever appeals to them?
9. Is it fair that numerous other nationalities refer to North Americans as having little or no self-control?

Babies are born with a self-centered and unruly tendency that, if not corrected, will cause much trouble. Proverbs 22:15 speaks about the way children are born: "Foolishness, (negative propensity) is bound in the heart of a child; but the rod of correction shall drive it far from him." Children are in desperate need of parents to guide them into disciplined adulthood.

10. Can parents build self-discipline into their children?
11. If parents have not given proper training, how can one acquire the necessary commitment and strength of character for self-discipline?

Christian stewardship requires diligent self-discipline and a willingness to learn. Proverbs 24:30-32 says, "I went by the field of the slothful, and by the vineyard of the man void of understanding; And, lo, it was all grown over with thorns, and nettles had covered the face thereof, and the stone wall thereof was broken down. Then I saw, and considered it well: I looked upon it, and received instruction."

12. Some people observe a situation and receive instruction from it; others see the same thing but completely miss the opportunity to learn from it. What makes the difference?

Fasting represents self-control by abstaining from the first and most basic need of man, which is food. The resolve and ability to plan and control your diet, and to practice periods of fasting will strengthen your ability to say no in other areas of life. Proverbs 25:16 has some instruction about self-control in this issue: "Hast thou found honey? Eat so much as is sufficient for thee, lest thou be filled therewith, and vomit it." Learning when to quit builds moral fiber that will help overcome other problems.

13. Can you by your own choice call yourself to a time of no food? (1 Cor. 7:5)
14. In the daily mealtime routine, can you "put a knife to your throat"? (Prov. 23:2)
15. Is your eating controlled by something more than your likes or dislikes?

The same is true concerning the tongue: James 3:2-b, "If any man offend not in word, the same is a perfect man, and able also to bridle the whole body." The necessity for tongue control, or more inclusive, communication control, has definitely been raised to new heights in recent years by the ever-increasing modern means of communication.

16. How does tongue-control relate to *whole body control*?
17. What is the meaning of "bridling" the body?
18. Does this bridling include controlling one's economic state of affairs?
19. Using a bridle as an illustration of control, think about who holds the reins?

Trouble-free times of abundance and easy credit are a definite hindrance to learning the character quality of enduring hardness as a good soldier. (2 Tim. 2:3)

20. What, if anything, can be done about this?

Galatians 6:5 relates to accountability. It says that "every man shall bear his own burden." This, of course, applies in many ways. In the context of this study, it means that when you assume a debt, you are accountable. When you accumulate various charges, you are accountable to pay them, not someone else. When you make commitments, you are responsible to keep them. It is not right to carelessly and knowingly get yourself into tight situations, and then expect people to come running to bail you out.

Also, be careful about trying to shift your expenses to other people, or the government, or even to your church. Neither government funds nor church funds are "free money." Someone had to pay taxes and give donations. Neither do insurance companies have free money; someone had to pay it.

21. What personal thoughts or experiences do you have to add to this subject?

Don't surrender your position of control; do not allow yourself to be brought under the power of your things and involvements. First Corinthians 6:12 says, "All things are lawful unto me, but all things are not expedient: all things are lawful for me, but I will not be brought under the power of any."

22. How can a person remain in control, especially in times of opportunity and prosperity?
23. Is it any different in times of economic recession or depression?

Consider these words of Jesus, "I pray not that thou shouldest take them out of the world, but that thou shouldest keep them from the evil. They are not of the world, even as I am not of the world. Sanctify them through thy truth: thy word is truth. As thou hast sent me into the world, even so have I also sent them into the world" (John 17:15-18).

24. How does God respond to this prayer of Jesus in the lives of Christians today?
25. Should we be able to sense the keeping power as we mingle with our fellow earthlings?

Before you wish for, or envy the circumstances of another person that you may think "has it made," you should consider all aspects of their circumstances and the full scope of their responsibilities. Their life might include things that you would be unwilling for, or even unable to cope with. Remember these words of Jesus; "For unto whomsoever much is given, of him shall be much required: and to whom men have committed much, of him they will ask the more" (Luke 12:48). With more means, comes more responsibility.

26. What should we wish for then?
27. In general, are one's circumstances and what is required of them usually balanced?

Get serious; don't expect to be frivolous and shallow, and yet to be successful in life. Titus 2: 6-7 says, "Young men likewise exhort to be sober minded. In all things showing thyself a pattern of good works: in doctrine showing uncorruptness, gravity, sincerity."

28. Do all young people have to in some way cross over the proverbial fool's hill before they can be sober and wise?

Honesty and integrity are a *must* for the Christian's success in life. Even though the word *honest* does not appear often in the King James Bible, the principle is scattered all through the Scriptures. We find one important reference in 1 Peter 2:11-12: "Dearly beloved, I beseech you as strangers and pilgrims, abstain from fleshly lusts, which war against the soul; Having your conversation honest among the Gentiles: that, whereas they speak against you as evildoers, they may by your good works, which they shall behold, glorify God in the day of visitation." Outright cheating or lying is usually not much of a temptation for sincere Christians, but it can become a test when it would be so easy to misrepresent something just a little bit, or to conceal a problem, and thereby realize economic gain.

This test becomes even more dangerous when another person requests your co-operation in a shady or dishonest deal, and your money is at stake. Sometimes they might only ask that you remain silent in some unethical transaction. You might be asked to "Just sign here, and tomorrow you can say, well, I changed my mind."

Total honesty may be regarded by some people as ridiculous or even a bit silly, but it's always the right plan to follow. And interestingly, even those people who scoff at others for practicing complete honesty want to be treated fairly and honestly though, when their money and things are at stake.

29. In the case of *silence only* on your part, does the guilt of wrongdoing lie all on the other person?
30. In the case of monetary mistakes or misdeeds, how small an amount of money is too little to bother correcting or calling to attention?
31. What is a *clear* conscience, and what is the value of it?
32. Is it true that a clear conscience allows people to sleep better?
33. How can it be that many wrongdoers rest well?

Beware of becoming "overcharged with the cares of this life" (Luke 21:34-36). This may be as simple as making too many commitments, trying to accomplish an excessive amount of things, or wanting to take advantage of too many desirable opportunities. By taking on too much, at some point one becomes weighed down or overburdened with excessive responsibilities and obligations. They may all be legitimate and acceptable in themselves; but by over-doing even good things, problems will result.

An old Chinese proverb relates to this verse. A man has too many pumpkins in the water, and he just can't keep them all together, so he ends up losing some. You may wonder why they had the pumpkins in the water in the first place. The same may be true about having too many cares: why did you make so many commitments, or purchase so many things in the first place?

The degree of required responsibilities or cares of life will by no means be the same for every person. People are diverse in their make-up, their personal circumstances and abilities are different, and their callings in life are not the same. To a large degree, spiritually and naturally, God sets these things in order as He sees fit, "dividing to every man severally as he will"(1 Cor. 12:11). Psalm 75:7 says more about it: "But God is the judge: he putteth down one, and setteth up another." Our challenge is to find a place that is right for us.

Most people will sooner or later have to learn the ability to pass up some desirable or even outstanding opportunities. David did this when he could have killed Saul, his enemy (1 Sam. 26:7-9). The spear was right there, waiting to be used; and his companion urged him to redeem the opportunity, even asserting that this was what God wanted him to do. David flatly declined, saying it was not right for him to do it. This kind of discernment and fortitude is imperative for success.

34. How can one have the strength to pass up opportunities that can look very good and therefore appear so right?
35. What does it take to withstand peer pressure in a direction that does not seem right or expedient?

Ponder the meaning of Luke 8:14, about being choked with cares, riches and pleasures of this life. Socially some people choke themselves with excessive commitments. Some have spiritually suffocating desires to be rich, perhaps very rich. Some get so caught up in pleasure seeking that there isn't time or mind space for spiritual things. Also in natural things, some people clutter their lives with so many things, gadgets and accessories that it makes their life cumbersome and can have a spiritually stifling effect. There are many other ways in which people overload themselves.

36. How can we discern when we are becoming overloaded with cares?
37. Is there a specific line for each person when enough is enough?
38. Is it possible to become so intent on finding and experiencing pleasures that in the end the person has little or no pleasure at all?

Purposely choosing to do without something that you would like to have, and could have, will be a real boost to your strength of self-discipline and will likely have a positive effect in greater and more important things in your life.

39. What would be some things with which to practice this virtue?

Give special attention to details; they can make the difference between success and failure. To a degree, many of the big issues either take care of themselves or force you to pay attention to them. However, small details may go unnoticed or seem unimportant and be neglected until they add up to a big sum which can easily push your budget into imbalance. If you skip a little here, lose a few tools there, spill something here and something there; if you tolerate a leak at one place and a little discrepancy in another place, sooner or later it will add up to a difficult struggle or even failure.

Here's an example of how diligence in small details can affect money management. It's important to pay your bills on time because sometimes, whether you like it or not, the discount you get for paying on time may be your only profit. Negligence in this detail may result in no profit at all. There are many other similar ways that small details can make a big difference.

In bygone years there were two farmers who lived and labored side by side. One was enjoying success, but the other one was in a constant struggle financially. One day as they each worked their soil, they met by the boundary of their fields. The struggling one inquired of the other one, "How do you make things work so well?" Mr. Success invited his neighbor to come over to his place in the evening after the work was finished, and "perhaps I can give you a few tips that will help you." When the struggling farmer arrived after dusk, he found his neighbor busy at his bookwork by the light of his kerosene lamp. Seeing his neighbor had arrived, Mr. Success said, "I will put out the lamp because we can talk just as well in the dark." The struggling farmer caught on immediately and responded, "Oh, just forget it. I'll be on my way home. I think I know how you do it."

40. Name some ways little details can have a big impact on the end results.

Sometimes people try to excuse themselves of their problems, saying that they lack in a necessary talent. Others struggle with envy because they notice those people who seem to be much more able to help themselves in life. Some may be satisfied with their level of performance when they shouldn't be. Whatever the case, there is a fairly simple way to acquire more talent. Use whatever talents you already have. How can this be true? "For unto every one that hath shall be given, and he shall have abundance: but from him that hath not shall be taken away even that which he hath" (Matt. 25:29).

41. Can you explain what it means to bury one's talent (Matt. 25:25)?
42. Do you know of any current-day occasions of talent re-distribution similar to verse 28?

Learn to resist persuasive sales pressures and convincing, but often deceptive advertisements. There are prizes to be won (they say) if you buy now, and all types of lures to make you want to buy. There are many people who want your money. It's up to you to understand where to spend, what to buy and not to buy, and when and where to give.

43. Is there a secret to being unaffected by the many sales gimmicks and tricks?
44. How can one say a firm no to sales pressures without being rude?

Because of a lack of personal discipline, far too many people live from paycheck to paycheck, barely making ends meet. This causes a situation similar to being a slave, always being forced by limits and deadlines. This often makes those people unavailable for service to others and for charity activities. If you live this way, others may often have to fill in the gaps you leave because you cannot to do your share.

45. Is it in order for family members or fellow church members to show concern if they see their kindred or peers living "from hand to mouth"?

Some people struggle to consistently apply the discipline to keep things under control and working. Sometimes some say they just get weary of the necessary restraint and feel like they can never enjoy any pleasures. They may ask, Must we always slave away at it? Can't we ever just cut loose, relax and just live?

46. What is the problem with such thoughts?
47. Can something be done to help such people to a better state of mind?

Ben Franklin said, "Early to bed and early to rise, makes a man healthy, wealthy and wise."

48. Is this statement true or false?
49. What is early, on time, or late for bedtime and arising?

Because of much social activity, many interests, and lack of self-discipline, or maybe because they are driven by their debts, many people do not get sufficient sleep. Few people have a problem of arising too early. Insufficient sleep is usually an evening problem. Proverbs 6:9-11, on the other hand, tells us about the morning problem: "How long wilt thou sleep, O sluggard? When wilt thou arise out of thy sleep? Yet a little sleep, a little slumber, a little folding of the hands to sleep: So shall thy poverty come as one that travelleth, and thy want as an armed man." Employers, schoolteachers and preachers are some of the people who see and feel the effects of inadequate sleep. It often has a negative effect in work performance and mental capacities on the job, as well as in general alertness, behavior and outlook in life.

50. What issues are involved in the discipline required to get the right amount of sleep?
51. How should one deal with cultural and community practices that keep one from getting enough sleep?

Always strive to be on time for work, for church and everything in between, even for your own goals. Being on time reduces stress and has many other advantages. It's a good habit.

Being late is a selfish and irresponsible habit, a bad one. Making others wait because you are late is like stealing their time. When one person makes six others wait for ten minutes, one whole hour is lost. When your tardiness costs other people money, it's equal to stealing their funds.

Allow a margin of time in your schedule. The person who usually plans to arrive right on the minute will often be late. Don't expect to be a habitual last-minute person and never suffer any consequences. Wisdom should give you a desire to rise above living on the edge, and perhaps usually "a day late and a dollar short," always in the red.

52. Is it still true that "The early bird gets the worm?"
53. How can habitual latecomers learn to be prompt?
54. If being prompt makes you stand out, what should you do about it?

Relating to another area of responsibility, 2 Kings 9:20 says about Jehu, that "he driveth furiously." A long time ago already people were known by their driving habits. It is so even today. What of the Christian?

Following are some slightly edited excerpts from a letter sent to young drivers by an auto insurance company in 1992. While not religious in content, it coincides with scriptural teaching on being responsible before God and accountable to other people as it relates to one's driving habits.

> You are receiving this letter because you are 23 years old or younger, the age group who tends to have the worst driving record of all groups.
>
> Young people normally have better eyesight, quicker reactions and more easily acquire other skills than older people and, therefore, should be our best drivers on the highway. Well, then, why are they the worst?
>
> One reason is that too many young drivers are bad drivers because they just haven't matured enough. They still think, act and react too much like children.
>
> Another apparent reason is the trait of youth that prompts one to *show off* and to *take chances* that most older people would shudder at.
>
> Here is a strange and puzzling fact. Young people usually take pride in their skill and abilities in many of their activities. Why then are so many so willing to prove their inability and incompetence when it comes to driving an automobile?
>
> Actually, it is more than just pride that should prompt you to drive safely and defensively instead of offensively. If you could see and experience the tragedies–brain damage, loss of limbs,

loss of sight, paralyzing spinal cord injuries, disfigurement, pain, suffering, and death—that our claim adjusters see in taking care of claims that are the result of too much speed, too much daring, carelessness, and inexperience; you could much better appreciate and understand why we are writing to you.

We appeal to you, for the sake of your own future, your own life, and the future and lives of others, to be wreck-less, not reckless; to be careful, not care-less; to demonstrate that youth can be trustworthy and not irresponsible.

It is true though, that not all young people are bad drivers. Some are model motorists. If you are, good! If you are not, hopefully you can be persuaded to learn to do the right, safe and sensible things when you take to the road.

55. Do you think driving practices have changed for the better since 1992?
56. In what way does this apply to people past age 23?

RECORD KEEPING

Another important aspect of responsible stewardship is keeping good records of your personal property and your financial activities and circumstances. Proverbs 27:23 says, "Be thou diligent to know the state of thy flocks, and look well to thy herds." It's about knowing what's going on with your things.

Luke 16:2 reads, "And he called him, and said unto him, How is it that I hear this of thee? give an account of thy stewardship; for thou mayest be no longer steward." In other words, bring your records; I want to see what's going on.

Although some people have good memories, very few can give an accurate account of their stewardship without written records. Good records require more than a computer and a checkbook. A good filing cabinet, properly managed, is a big help in finding information and accounts when you need them.

Basic record categories include

- Legal documents of all types, government papers, health records, etc.

- Mortgage or loan agreements, and other long-term commitments.
- Real-estate deeds and property-cost records, car and truck titles, etc.
- Income and expense records of personal finances, and business if applicable.
- Owner's manuals, warranty papers, purchase receipts, etc.
- Service records for cars, machinery, appliances and such-like.
- Any important personal information and statistics.

There are good reasons for accurate financial record keeping.

- For your own knowledge of your personal finances
- To know where your income will come from and how much to expect
- To know where you expect to spend, how much, and for what
- To meet the government requirement for income tax purposes, etc.
- To understand your circumstances and manage your business
- To show prospective buyers a history of profits if you ever sell the business

It is never too soon for young people to start keeping financial records. When you open a checking account, reconcile your checkbook balance with your bank statement to the penny. If it doesn't balance, find out what's wrong. Know where you are. It will have an overall positive impact on your finances. Young people who keep adequate records generally find it easier to discipline themselves to a successful lifestyle.

Though some people do have excellent mental capacities, there is no substitute for accurate, explainable and well-kept records. A computer is not an automatic remedy for bad record keeping. How your desktop looks now is probably the way the inside of your computer will look. Computers require as much discipline as a ledger book does, or more.

Romans 12:11 says we should "not be slothful in business." The necessary diligence is usually time well invested. If you can't do it yourself, it usually pays to hire a bookkeeper.

Careful record keeping will have a positive effect toward your success and will facilitate a proper sense of accomplishment. It's better to keep more papers than actually necessary than to throw something out too quickly and find out later that you still needed it.

1. What effect, if any, do good records have on charitable giving?
2. What should you do if you are keeping good records and they reveal problems?
3. To whom, and to what extent, are youth and young couples accountable concerning their finances?
4. Are those who are no longer youth or young couples accountable or responsible to anyone?

TRAINING YOUR FAMILY TO BE RESPONSIBLE

Many well-meaning parents do everything for their small children, pick up after them, clean up for them, and much more. Some continue to do this as the children grow older and in the end they produce irresponsible children. This can also happen in other ways as children become adults. If your children are spoiled brats, think real hard about whose fault it is. Proverbs 29:15 and 17 says, "The rod and reproof give wisdom: but a child left to himself (*or catered to*), bringeth his mother to shame. Correct thy son, and he shall give thee rest; yea, he shall give delight unto thy soul."

When children have a financial responsibility to the parents, or even to other people, some parents too readily say, "Oh, just forget it," or "Oh, well, we'll just pay it for you," or "You can just have it." By doing such things too frequently, even though well meant, the parents can unintentionally foster irresponsibility in their children.

Their children might even begin to presume on this practice, thinking, Oh well, dad will probably let it go; or, Mom will probably pay for it; or, our parents will most likely forgive our debt; or they may assume that because nothing is said, everything is acceptable as it is. In the course of time, these kinds of things often result in serious problems for both the parents and their children.

Parents should rather do their children a favor and require them to be accountable and responsible for their own debts, in a real-life manner. If you want to give them a lift in life, it is better to give them an outright gift, than to let too many things slide into grey zones where nobody knows what is what.

1. Can parents do any backtracking in this area if they see failure in their practices?

2. Can parents, or children, easily become too zealous in keeping track of every little detail of who is responsible for what, who owes whom, how much, and for what?

Sometimes people fear responsibility, perhaps due to feelings of inferiority, a lack of proper self-confidence, or for other reasons. This can cause a person to languish in the shadows and remain unproductive in life. Yet, willingness to assume responsibility, whether it is voluntary, delegated, or even by coercion, is a big part of the making of a person of value and promotes fiber in one's character.

3. What can parents go by, to know when it's time to start assigning responsibility to their children, and how much they can handle?
4. Are affluent circumstances a hindrance to this issue?

Often in life one thing is a sign of another. It has been said that cluttered houses, workshops, vehicles and purses, etc. are signs of an undisciplined life. Even crumpled and dog-eared money in your wallet is probably a sign, at least to some degree, of an unorganized life.

5. Do you think these thoughts are correct? If so, are there are exceptions?
6. Can anyone actually, by choice, change in these things?
7. What is wrong when a person plans to change, tomorrow?

Church staff members will need to need to beware of feeling like a dictator when they are giving help and advice on these issues. They are, after all, not the boss. First Peter 5:3 says, "Neither as being lords over *God's* heritage, but being ensamples to the flock."

On the other hand, it is not a small matter to lightly dismiss the counsel or advice of a faithful, dedicated deacon or pastor. Headstrong and willful persistence in one's ideas in spite of contrary advice is like asking for trouble. Inviting advice goes a long way in avoiding the school of hard knocks.

8. How can youth (and older people) learn the value of asking for advice and counsel; and then use it?

Peer pressure and cultural demands can be powerful forces and can put lots of stress in your life and on your finances. You may at times feel a strong urge or pressure to buy an item mostly because it seems like "everyone else" has one; or you may be tempted to try to make an impression, or a self-promoting "identity statement." This is especially true if you are not grounded in practice and in a sense of direction for your own goals in life.

It can seem quite important to get the "right" clothing and accessories for certain occasions, etc. You may feel inferior if you don't serve on par meals, of just the right menu, served on the right dinnerware, regardless of what it costs. You may feel pressured to have a vehicle of a certain manufacturer, or certain brands of house furnishings, clothing, tools, or equipment. You really do need your own convictions and strength of character to do what you know to be right for you.

Close to Pincher Creek, Alberta, there is a park called Head-Smashed-In Buffalo Jump. The interpretive center explains that the Indians hunted buffalo by stampeding the animals. By guiding the lead buffalos, they could send the herd galloping off a high cliff, thereby providing themselves a bountiful harvest of buffalo.

Unfortunately, sometimes people behave like buffalos as they unthinkingly follow each other and obtusely proceed over an allegorical cliff. Don't be like a buffalo, blindly dashing after the crowd. Instead, think like Joshua, who told the people that regardless of what they would do, or who they were going to choose to follow, "as for me and my house, we will serve, (or follow) the Lord (not the crowd)" (Josh. 24:15).

9. What is the right mind-set to "dare to be a Daniel," or a Joshua?
10. How can one be a Daniel and yet meekly and humbly blend in with his peers?
11. Is there much danger of becoming too strong a Daniel?

In real life it is usually not workable or acceptable to travel to every wedding and reception, reunion, or social function that you are invited to. The invitations may be quite persuasive, or even coërcive: please do come, they might say. But you are the one who will be taking off from work, (thereby shrinking your paycheck), and normally you are the one that will pay for the associated cost. Without a personal fortitude and sense of direction, peer pressure or your own desires can readily overshadow common sense and better knowledge, causing you to spend even when you shouldn't, or when you can't afford it.

12. Where and how does the example of parents fit into this issue of guiding their children to common sense decisions?
13. What is *a strong personal constitution*, and how does one acquire it?

When the time comes for young Christian people to think about companionship for life, it is important to be very prayerful about the issue. Young people should have a live desire for God's direction for this step in life and be open for His direction. Even so, it is in order to consider character qualities and personal circumstances.

Young man, it is altogether acceptable for a young lady to care about your lifestyle and how you do business and manage your finances. Does it look like you are a responsible steward with your money? Do you appear to be a real Christian with convictions and a spiritual sense of direction? Her parents also are allowed to consider whether you appear to be a trustworthy Christian man to whom they can comfortably entrust their daughter. Do you appear to have what it takes to support a wife and a family?

Likewise, young lady, that young man may consider if you appear to be a chaste and spiritual young woman. Does it look like you have what it takes to be an able, thrifty and trustworthy homemaker? He may consider whether you appear to be a good helper at home, or if you are loafing and carousing your way into womanhood without learning the responsibilities of a wife and mother. He may consider whether you appear to know how to handle money, or whether you would drain the checkbook. His parents also may consider if you would appear to be a good wife for their son.

Yes, you can change after you get married, but generally what you are now, is what you will tend to be then. So it becomes very important that you learn now to be what you should be as a spouse and companion. Although the spiritual side of life is of foremost importance, the practical side of everyday life is also very important.

This places a weighty responsibility on parents to train up their children with those virtues and qualities that will make them good spouses when they are grown and on their own.

14. Parents, are you preparing them with what they will need for real life?
15. What honest thoughts, questions, or experiences do you have to share about this issue?
16. How can young people best help themselves if they realize they are deficient in these things?
17. What should parents do, if their children are already grown, and then they realize that they have missed the mark in preparing them for the responsibilities and challenges of married life?

SOW A THOUGHT, AND REAP AN ACT;
SOW AN ACT, AND REAP A HABIT;
SOW A HABIT, AND REAP A CHARACTER;
SOW A CHARACTER, AND REAP A DESTINY.
—*ANONYMOUS*

The Work Ethic

CHAPTER7

Work is right. Work is good and beneficial. God expects people to work. We read about this already in Genesis 2:15: "The Lord God took the man, and put him into the Garden of Eden to dress it and to keep it."

Second Thessalonians 3:10 gives some pointed teaching on this: "For even when we were with you, this we commanded you, that if any would not work, neither should he eat. For we hear that there are some which walk among you disorderly, working not at all, but are busybodies. Now them that are such we command and exhort by our Lord Jesus Christ, that with quietness they work, and eat their own bread." Here we see that work and food normally go together, and indolence is disorderly.

Further, Ecclesiastes 11:4 and 6 says, "He that observeth the wind shall not sow; and he that regardeth the clouds shall not reap. . . . In the morning sow thy seed, and in the evening withhold not thine hand: for thou knowest not whether shall prosper, either this or that, or whether they both shall be alike good." Again it appears that labor and food go hand in hand. In addition we see that one should not excuse himself because circumstances look unfavorable or because one cannot see how things will turn out.

1. Does this mean that one needs to launch out somewhat blindly?
2. Can anyone actually find joy in manual labor?

One dictionary definition for *work ethic* is "a set of values based on the moral virtues of hard work and diligence."

In the North American culture the work ethic has been weakening. To a large degree this may be due to good times and a strong economy, which seem to have brought about a softening with every succeeding generation. But regardless of the times or current circumstances in our lives, knowing *how to work* is still a very good education. It is of top priority for making your way in life. Beyond that, one must learn to see the work and its necessity. Self-starter employees will always be sought after and appreciated. An anonymous quote says, "The only place success comes before work is in the dictionary."

It takes investment of time, effort, sacrifice and often money for parents to successfully teach this lesson. The ongoing, daily responsibility of chores is of great present and future value to growing children. Thomas Huxley (1825-1875) said, "Perhaps the most valuable result of education is the ability to make yourself do the thing you have to do, when it ought to be done, whether you like it or not."

Applying oneself to diligent, hard work promotes good health, a sense of well being, and a healthy self-respect. It gives you satisfaction and contentment that cannot be gained by idleness or lethargy. Vigorous physical labor is good for the mind and strengthens the body and the soul. Plus, it usually fills the wallet.

Some years ago a couple was poised to make a move out of their new house, away from the husband's good job, and into an old farmhouse on a dairy farm where the husband would work as a general laborer for farm wages. When the wife was asked if she thought it would work, she answered, "We think it will, but money is not the focal point. We want to be together as a family and teach our children how to work." Time proved that it did work and the children did learn how to work and provide for themselves.

3. Can you give some practical advice about how parents can teach their children a good work ethic in this pushbutton and automated, pre-programmed era?
4. What should parents do if they realize that they will have less than the best, sometimes even unacceptable results, if they give their children a job?
5. Is it acceptable to be a willing worker, only to the extent that one is motivated by necessity?
6. How can parents best teach their children a willingness to work?

7. Do children just automatically adopt their parent's mind-set and example on work?
8. What does it really mean to "*earn* a living"?

Acts 17:21 speaks of people who were more interested in talking than working. Proverbs 14:23 says, "In all labour there is profit: *but the talk of the lips tendeth only to penury.*" The problem of too much talk and not enough work has not gone away with the passing of time. Instead, due to our current high-tech communication, this problem seems to be intensifying. Communication is good, but there is a time to talk and a time to be quiet (and work). See Ecclesiastes 3:7. Good work performance and much talk generally are not compatible. If you don't agree, you may want to ask your boss about this subject.

Luke 10:38-42 tells the story about Mary and Martha, when Jesus came visiting. This parable has things to say about visiting and working. Martha apparently was overly concerned about preparations and serving, but surely she was not all wrong, and maybe Mary was not all right. In real life someone does need to prepare meals and serve them. This issue then, leaves us with a few questions.

9. Are there any simple rules that tell us when it is time to visit and when it is time to work?
10. Was Jesus perhaps teaching that people tend to put too much emphasis on meals, and not enough on true communication and learning?
11. Are there times when we should override normal common sense practices for the sake of visiting?

In 1 Timothy 5:8, we read about the person who might be willingly and busily at work, but for whatever reason, is not willing to provide for members of his own family. It is actually speaking about the care of widows in the family. It says, "But if any provide not for his own, and specially for those of his own house, he hath denied the faith, and is worse than an infidel." It may be that this also applies to a person who is not willing to work to procure the necessary provisions for his family.

12. What thoughts do you have about this issue?

Now let us consider a few thoughts about how much to work. Exodus 20:9 says, Six days shalt thou labour, and do all thy work; *six*; not five and not seven. In North America times have been so good for so long, that many people consider Saturday a day for recreation. It is naturally so, that if the father is gone five days a week on the job, Saturday, when he is home should be a special day. However, we do not find support in the Scriptures for one play day a week.

13. If you think seriously about it, what do you think will, in the long run, make father's day off the job most rewarding?
14. And what about youth?

It is good for children to develop a "self-starter" ambition already in their young years. For success, people first need to see the work and then put themselves to the task.

It is necessary, however, to find an effective Christian balance between work, family, church, etc. It takes some planning to find that balance. You may find it helpful to use a planning calendar or other methods to plan your days and manage your time.

If you realize that you lack ambition and motivation, whatever the reason, you can still learn by strict self-discipline and purpose. Strive to be like Nehemiah's co-workers: They built the wall with good progress, "for the people had a mind to work" (Neh. 4:6). Acquiring a good work ethic is closely tied to practical perseverance and persistence. This is the ability, among other things, to stick to a job and finish it, whether it's desirable or not. Such tenacity will carry over into many other areas of life. Here again, parents have a big responsibility to instill this quality into their children.

15. Can parents do anything to instill tenacity in their children after they are grown?
16. Is tenacity always a virtue, or can it at times become a hindrance?

In North America today, there is an epidemic of diabetes and other illnesses. Supposedly a major reason for this is that most people no longer get sufficient exercise because so many things are powered and automated. Perhaps we are a spoiled and soft generation.

So now many folks are spending money at exercise clubs. Some buy exercise machines. Ironically, many of these are powered machines. Many of these exercise apparatuses soon end up unused or in storage because they require too much effort and self-discipline.

17. How can we best be helped in this issue?
18. Should we deliberately choose to un-power some things to help ourselves?
19. Should we be more willing to earn our way by the sweat of our brow?

Work is good and necessary, but due to the weakness of humanity, it is also imperative to stay on guard against the danger of becoming a workaholic. Don't *over* work; there is a common sense time to quit. This obviously is more of a problem for some people than for others. Proverbs 23:4 relates to erroneous work aspirations: "Labour not to be rich: cease from thine own wisdom." This verse refers to being mentally and physically driven by an inordinate desire to attain and to be rich.

Be careful not to fall into bondage to your occupation or business, always being driven to accomplish and acquire more and yet more. Remember that God is well able to have the last word in your endeavors and to shape the end results as He sees fit.

On the other side of the issue, some people make many excuses for not applying themselves. This is not a new problem. Proverbs 20:4 says, "The sluggard will not plow by reason of the cold; therefore shall he beg in the harvest, and have nothing."

In bygone years there were numerous men (and a few ladies) roaming the countryside, begging for food and lodging, some because they were unwilling to work. One such character sat in the shade watching a group of men labor in the hot sun to harvest a field of grain. He tauntingly told them, "It sure is nice when one has nothing. See, I don't have to work and sweat in the heat like you do." But later as the laborers washed up to enjoy a good meal, he wanted to be included. Then he said, "It would be nice if one had a little something." He was literally *begging in the harvest*, because he had not been willing to apply himself beforehand.

Today yet, some people have their excuses for working very little or not at all. Others have their reasons or justifications for working far too much.

20. Who is qualified to say what is balanced?
21. What criterion gives one direction or authority for teaching or reproof on this matter?
22. Might the answer depend on varying economic conditions?

Proverbs 6:6-11 says, "Go to the ant, thou sluggard; consider her ways, and be wise: Which having no guide, overseer, or ruler, Provideth her meat in the summer, *and* gathereth her food in the harvest. How long wilt thou sleep, O sluggard? When wilt thou arise out of thy sleep? Yet a little sleep, a little slumber, a little folding of the hands to sleep: So shall thy poverty come as one that travelleth, and thy want as an armed man." In other words, Discipline yourself, get up and get going; or sleep too much and be poor.

23. Is this just a morning problem, or is it directly related to the discipline of the evening before?
24. How much might the parents be at fault if their children have this problem?

Whether or not you can accomplish difficult tasks or assignments depends a lot on your state of mind. Proverbs 23:7 applies to this issue. It says; "For as he thinketh in his heart, so is he." This agrees with the saying, Whether you think you can or you can't, either way you are probably correct. The following account illustrates this.

A young man eagerly took a job in a car repair shop. One day he was asked to remove a smashed fender from a car. After working at it for a period of time, perhaps halfheartedly, he told his boss, "I cannot get the smashed fender off." "Well," said the boss, "if you can't get the fender off, you can't work here." He really did want the job. The fender came off. A new mind-set made all the difference!

Romans 12:11 tells us that we are to be "not slothful in business, fervent in spirit." This speaks about an up-beat, can-do state of mind.

25. Is the right mind-set a matter of choice?
26. Can parents build it into their children? If so, how?
27. Does temperament ever justify faulty reasoning?

Procrastination can be a real enemy for some people. An old adage says, "Tomorrow, tomorrow, but not today; that's what the lazy people say." If you have a problem in this line, keep a to-do list and make yourself do it. Enlist the support of others. Another helpful thing is to "brighten the corner" where you work. A clean, organized work place improves efficiency and morale.

28. How could one solicit the support of others to become more diligent?
29. Is a disorganized work place always a detriment to productivity? For all people?

To make things work and to succeed in life and your occupation, realistic ideas and goals with consistent actions are very important. When it's time to consider a variety of options, keep this in mind: Nothing is so good that there is no chance of failure, and few things are so bad that there is no chance of success with the proper approach and know-how. To make a choice among available opportunities, consider the options and outlook, ask advice, and then make a decision, do away with the alternatives and stick with your decision. In other words, do your best to give your efforts a fair chance to succeed.

30. When it comes to achieving success, is it true that God helps those who help themselves?
31. Are some people born, as Is sometimes said, "with a silver spoon in their mouth," or does it just seem that way to the onlookers?

When it's time to go job hunting or to choose an occupation or business venture, consider your motives and your attitude and what you are looking for and why. Not all jobs or occupations are acceptable for Christian people. Titus 3:14 says that Christians should "maintain good works for necessary uses." It is essential to use the proper priorities to evaluate your opportunities. Following is a suggested list of priorities.

- Earning a living. (Remember, if any does not work . . .)
- Preserving your Christian family order.
- Being a Christian witness on the job, or through your business associations.
- Being of use to man, working a job of honorable and upright service.
- Learning a trade of necessary and respectable service.

32. What else belongs in the list, or in what order should the list be?
33. How would you explain *necessary uses* in Titus 3:14?

Most times it's not wise to wait around for the highest paying or the most ideal job or business opportunity. The usual results of foregoing available opportunities in hopes of perfect conditions are listed in Ecclesiastes 11:4. "He that observeth the wind shall not sow; and he that regardeth the clouds shall not reap." Verse 6 says: "In the morning sow thy seed, and in the evening withhold not thine hand: for thou knowest not whether shall prosper, either this or that, or whether they both shall be alike good." In other words, start where you are and redeem the opportunity at hand, even though it might not be exactly what you prefer. Proverbs 10:5 says, "He that gathereth in summer is a wise son." If you want to be wise, gather (or work) at the right time and when the opportunity is present.

Americans tend to be "soft," self-centered people, desiring to have things easy and just the way they like it. Don't just think of finding what you like to do, or what you think fits your dream in every way. Bible principles teach us that it is not acceptable to always want the easiest job, the best pay, and the most desirable circumstances.

A man of the past was telling his younger brothers-in-law about the virtues of his job. After enumerating all the good things about the job, he added, "Oh, it's hard work, but I like it." In its proper place and with the right attitude, it is possible yet today to actually enjoy hard physical labor.

34. How can parents train their children to cheerfully take a less-than-best job if it's good for now or if that's all that's available?
35. Is there a way to help those who think that a job with lower-than-desired pay is not even worth taking?

When choosing an occupation, paychecks and potential profits may be considered, but dollars should never be the Christian's number one priority. The ability to maintain a solid family structure should be given a high priority. If one has the right state of mind, there is a wide range of respectable jobs that can be a genuine blessing to you, your family, and your fellow people. Look for a job or an occupation that can serve as a platform from which to serve the Lord even as you earn your livelihood. It is a wise idea to ask the Spirit of God to help you prove what is acceptable to the Lord.

36. How does Ephesians 5:8-11 relate to occupation choices?
37. Should one allow other people to help prove which occupations are acceptable?

It should be the goal of Christian fathers to be at home with their family as much as possible. A man, who was on the way home from his job, stopped at a grocery store. He stated that because his place of employment was very busy, they were begging for people to work overtime. When he was asked if he was working long hours to earn an extra big paycheck, he responded, "No way! I have four boys at home, and they are only going to grow up once, and I'm going to be there." This is an excellent ideal for every father; wanting to be present and involved as the family grows up.

As soon as possible and as much as is expedient, involve your children in whatever work there is for them to do, whether in home-keeping or a livelihood occupation, or other options of honorable value. The family that works together has a good thing going for them.

38. To what degree should fathers forego wages or profits to be at home more?
39. Can you name some of the values and blessings of fathers spending time at home and families working together?

Sometimes people take a dim view of common labor. But a diligent laborer deserves much credit; don't look down on him as if he is filling only a lowly place. It is true that often someone, perhaps somewhere in an office, needs to plan and oversee the project; but it's the laborer that actually makes things happen. For this there should be proper respect and perhaps more people willing to get dirty hands. "But rather let him labour, *working with his hands* the thing which is good" (Eph. 4:28).

40. Should everyone be willing to start at the bottom?
41. Does anyone ever rise to a position of being above the injunction of *working with his hands*?

Ephesians 4:28 addresses yet other reasons to be a willing worker: "Let him that stole steal no more: but rather let him labour, working with his hands the thing which is good, that he may have to give to him that needeth." We should work and earn the means for our needs, so we won't be tempted to steal our necessities, and so we can even have some to give to others in need.

42. Is stealing often the result of an unwillingness to work?
43. Can most everyone attain an attitude of working cheerfully for the purpose of giving? Following are a few more items related to work, for food for thought.

"The reward for man's toil is not what he gets for it, but what he becomes by it" (John Ruskin).

ONE HUNDRED PERCENTER'S CREED

Today Is The Very First Day Of The Rest Of My Life
This is the beginning of a new day.
I have been given this day to use as I will.
I can waste it...or use it for good. But what I do today is important,
because I am exchanging a day of my life for it!
When tomorrow comes, this day will be gone forever,
leaving in its place something that I have traded for it.
I want it to be gain, and not loss; good and not evil;
success and not failure;
in order that I shall not regret the price that I have paid for it.
I will give 100% of myself just for today,
for you never fail until you stop trying.
—Anonymous

THE GREATEST REMEDY

Work is man's greatest function. He is nothing, he can do nothing, he can achieve nothing, fulfill nothing, without work.

If you are poor, work. If you are rich, continue working. If you are burdened with seemingly unfair responsibilities, work. If you are happy, keep right on working. Idleness gives room for doubts and fears. If disappointments come, work. When faith falters, work. When dreams are shattered and hopes seem dead, work. No matter what ails you, work.

It is the greatest remedy available for both mental and physical afflictions. The better way.

–Author unknown

Although the Bible is the final authority on this and all subjects, there is much to be said in favor of willing, hard work, and perhaps even unwilling work.

Because of humanity's problems, it may be that the best impetus for work and exercise is conditions and circumstances that cause the necessity of it.

Good work ethics cannot be bought, traded or sold. They can however, be implanted, taught and learned.

44. What summarizing thoughts do you have to share about work?

Considerations for Employers

CHAPTER 8

Being an employer is serious business and carries a great deal of responsibility. It requires much self-discipline and even self-sacrifice. An employer who has the right attitude is more like a servant than like one being served. He serves others by supplying a job, training, and a livelihood. A good employer thinks more of having his employees working *with* him than *for* him.

1. When an employer hires someone, how responsible does he become for the employee?
2. Can you explain the difference between working with an employer and working for him?

If you are an employer, or planning to become one, you should consider whether you are doing it only for your own advantage or also for the benefit of the employee. Self-centered thoughts can cause lots of employer and employee problems. Philippians 2:4 instructs us to "Look not every man (*only*) on his own things, but every man also on the things of others."

3. Can you name some practical ways to apply this to employers?

It should be an important goal for Christian employers to be pleasant to work for. We could re-word Romans 13:9-b, 10 a bit and say, "Thou shalt love thy neighbour (*employee*) as thyself. (*Because*) Love worketh no ill to his neighbour (*employee*): therefore love is the fulfilling of the law." Unfortunately some employees are harder to appreciate than others, but if you love only the ideal employee, "what do you more than others?" See Matthew 5:43-48.

4. Is this Bible standard attainable or just an ideal to strive for?
5. How can the boss learn to like the less likeable employee?

Another important qualification for an employer is integrity. General surveys about employers have shown that total trustworthiness is the number one quality desired by employees. Generally, even ungodly people desire leaders with integrity. Uprightness and integrity is taught all through the Bible for all people, but it's especially pertinent for good employers, bosses and leaders in general.

6. How would you explain the term integrity as it relates to employers?
7. Is there such a thing as *total integrity* or is it just an ideal?

Employers, remember the Golden Rule. If you practice the Golden Rule on the job, you can avoid many problems. Exercise a care and concern for the well being of your employee, like the centurion did for his servant (Matt. 8:5-18). And try to always remember the law of sowing and reaping (Gal. 6:7).

8. How does Galatians 6:9, 10 apply to this subject?

A good employer should not need to hustle about frantically or bossily, coercing his employees to perform according to his expectations. Under normal circumstances, if there is a proper foundation, he should be able to guide with composed instruction, a calm tip here and a gentle tap there. A humble willingness to address potential problems with straightforward, yet kind, honesty before they become a big dilemma is much better than waiting until dire circumstances occur. An old saying declares that "an ounce of prevention is worth a pound of cure." There is lots of truth to that.

9. Must this type of leadership be learned, or is it God-given to some people?
10. Can you share an example or an experience of a good employer or boss that would illustrate these qualities?

Employers and bosses or job foremen must always strive to be sensible and fair. The slave days are supposed to be past. Be good to your employees and restrain yourself from harsh requirements or mistreatment. "And, ye masters . . . *forbearing threatening*: knowing that your Master also is in heaven; neither is there respect of persons with him"(Eph. 6:9). Sometimes masters forget that they themselves have a Master of masters over them. As the boss or foreman, you have authority over your subordinates, but you are not in ultimate control. "To his own master he stands or falls" (Rom. 14:4). It is in order to be careful in your demands and judgments of your employees.

11. Should it seem somewhat scary to be an employer?

Don't let your position as employer or foreman go to your head. Romans 12:3 cautions, "For I say . . . to every man that is among you, not to think of himself *more highly than he ought to think*; but to think soberly." Due to the depraved nature of man, this is not a useless warning. Any person in authority needs to be careful not to look down on those over whom he has authority. Furthermore, an employer should be careful not to demand more of his employees than he is willing to do himself.

When George Washington was general of the U.S. Army, he came upon a scene where a commander, much beneath him in authority, was having his men load a heavy log onto a wagon. Seeing that they were not quite able to accomplish the task, even though the commander was shouting commands and encouragement, George stepped up and assisted the men, and the log was loaded onto the wagon. George then instructed their commander not just to stand there shouting at his men, but to help them. Not realizing who George was, the man said, "Oh, but I am the commander." And George Washington's response? "Well, then, call me. I am the General."

12. Can you share any current-day examples that relate to the above subject?
13. May the boss ever, for right reasons, expect the employee to do the hard or dirty work?

For over-all, long-term success, employers usually need to be humble enough to delegate responsibility to their employees, at least to some degree. To instill incentive and a sense of being needed, it is wise to include the employee in management and operation decisions when it's practical. Consider Jethro's advice to his father-in-law, Moses. See Exodus 18:13-23.

14. What is the problem if an employer can't ever delegate any responsibility or authority to his employees?
15. If the employees seem to all be viewed as inept or unskilled, is there a problem with the boss? If so, what might it be?

Mr. Boss, it's a good virtue to learn from your employees. Listen to their ideas and suggestions. Ecclesiastes 4:9 states that "two are better than one, because they have a good reward for their labor." The employer must never think that he is altogether self-sufficient or that he knows it all and that he needs the help of no one.

16. An old adage says that two heads are better than one, even if one is a cabbage head. Is it true? If so, what is the moral of it?

Beware of undue suspicions toward your employees. They can easily ruin the day. Some say, he who does not trust, cannot be trusted. If you want your employees to trust you, you must trust them unless they prove to be untrustworthy. There is a similar thought in Proverbs 18:24: "A man that hath, (*or wants*) friends must show himself friendly." Generally, if you trust others, you will gain their trust in return.

17. Is there a danger of trusting one's employees too much?
18. How can an employer re-gain betrayed trust?

In real life, your employees will make mistakes, sometimes serious and costly ones. And sometimes employees are inconsiderate and not as loyal as they should be. They may fail in a wide variety of ways. All this calls for communication, tolerance and forgiveness. It's good to remember that most likely you have also made some serious mistakes yourself.

19. What should an employer do when an employee fails to admit his mistake and take responsibility for it?

20. What should the boss do with the employee who repeatedly makes the same mistake?
21. What should an employer do if an employee takes days off, time and again, at the drop of a hat, perhaps without even asking?
22. Do employers need an extra measure of ability to forgive?

A good boss or employer must do more than attain a title. You need to give your employees good reasons to look up to you in the area of character and performance. Endeavor to be a devout leader with purpose and character, one who is worth following.

Schoolteachers are not employers, but much of this chapter also applies to them. The same can be said for many other occupations or professions in life.

23. Are there any shortcuts, or are the right qualities only gained by experience and time?

A good employer or boss also needs to feel and express appreciation for a job well done, and for faithful, long-term service by the employee.

An employer, talking to a friend about one of his employees, said, "He is such a good employee, that I just cannot do enough for him." On another day that very employee was visiting with the same man, and knowing nothing about what his employer had told the man, said almost the same words about his boss, "He is such a good boss. He treats me so well that I just can't do enough for him." These men certainly had a good thing going and were both winners.

24. How can such an attitude be attained?

Now comes the paying part of being an employer. The Bible has lots of teaching about this subject. As an employer you have a lot of control of this issue, but it should be your policy to pay fair wages and do it on time, gladly and cheerfully, because in Luke 10:7 it says, "The laborer is worthy of his hire (*or paycheck*)," and again in 1 Timothy 5:18, "The laborer is worthy of his reward." Colossians 4:1 tells how much to pay an employee: "Masters, give unto your servants that which is just and equal; knowing that ye also have a Master in heaven."

Fortunate indeed, are the employees who have an employer who honestly finds it a pleasure to pay his employees, fairly and generously.

25. What criteria should employers go by to decide what pay scale is *just and equal*?
26. Is it scripturally required, or should it at least be possible for an employer to actually enjoy paying his employees their wages? Is there a secret for how to accomplish this?
27. What shall an employer do, if because of good business, a promised profit-share or any similar bonus, is much larger than he anticipated?

One more very important issue about paychecks is to pay promptly and on time, according to your agreement. This was a requirement in the Old Testament law. "Thou shalt not oppress an hired servant that is poor and needy, whether he be of thy brethren, or of thy strangers that are in thy land within thy gates: At his day thou shalt give him his hire, neither shall the sun go down upon it; for he is poor, and setteth his heart upon it: lest he cry against thee unto the Lord, and it be sin unto thee" (Deut. 24:14-15). This makes paying the right amount, at the right time imperative.

The New Testament has an admonition about holding back rightfully due wages. "Behold, the hire of the labourers who have reaped down your fields, *which is of you kept back by fraud*, crieth: and the cries of them which have reaped are entered into the ears of the Lord of sabaoth" (James 5:4).

28. Why might an employer withhold due pay?
29. Do tight funds exonerate an employer from the guilt of paying late?
30. What is an employee supposed to do if he is not being paid enough, or not at the appointed time?
31. Do you have any concluding thoughts, or positive illustrations about employers?

Instructions for Employees

CHAPTER 9

To be an employee and have a job is a privilege, something to be thankful for. To be able to work and have an occupation and to earn your necessities in life is a blessing. To be able to be a giver from your earnings is yet another advantage.

To be employed as a laboring servant and work at an honorable job is not an inferior position. Willing workers deserve much credit. If you are, or expect to be an employee, hopefully this study will encourage the state of mind that allows the blessing of God on your workdays.

In order to qualify as a good employee, perhaps the first thing to consider is respect for your employer. The Scriptures teach that you need to be submissive and respectful to your boss, whether he is of noble character or perchance unreasonable. "Servants, be subject to your masters with all fear; not only to the good and gentle, but also to the froward" (1 Pet. 2:18). To get the real picture, read on to the end of 1 Peter 2. It is sometimes astounding what positive effects a godly employee can have on a "froward," or strong-willed, contrary boss.

1. What might be the problem if it is a constant trial to be compliant and respectful to the boss?
2. Does God impart a special grace to work for difficult employers?

For practical, honorable and down-to-earth jobs, employers are often not seriously concerned about what degrees you hold or how much knowledge you have. They are more interested in whether you are trainable and know how to work. People who apply themselves to their work according to Bible principles are usually sought after and appreciated as employees. This is usually true even of those employers who give little or no recognition to God and the Bible.

3. With what attitude then, should one approach a potential job interview?

Christian people should always want to be known as diligent, dependable, trustworthy, and honest. Not only are they right qualities, but these four points are also always in demand by employers.

An old story illustrates these virtues. It occurred years ago when it was still legal to employ quite young boys. A drug store owner wanted a dependable and honest young boy to help in his store after school, so he hung a sign in the window: Boy Wanted.

When a young lad came in and inquired about the job, the owner took him to a back room and showed him a wooden box filled with screws and nails. He instructed the young lad to sort them out, "then come and tell me when you are finished." The boy got discouraged before he was finished, told the owner he did not want the job after all, and left.

A second young lad came and was given the same assignment. After just a few minutes he changed his mind and didn't want the job after all.

A third boy was given the same assignment. He finished the job and invited the owner to come and look whether he had done the job correctly. When the boss gave his approval of the job well done, the boy withdrew something from his pocket saying; "And look what I found in the bottom of the box." He showed the owner a five dollar gold coin. The boss had placed it there as a test of honesty.

The first two boys were not diligent, dependable, nor honest, because they both didn't finish the job, plus they both stole the coin. The third boy had all four qualities. He was diligent, dependable, trustworthy, and honest, and he got the job.

Later, the employer purposely left increasing amounts of money where he knew his new employee would find it, to see what he would do. The young man passed the tests and was promoted to a very responsible position.

Employees with this four-point character are still in great demand, and it should be the goal of all Christian parents to send their children forth, thus taught and equipped for work and for life.

Titus 2:9, 10 gives more instruction: "Exhort servants (*employees*) to be obedient to their own masters, to be well pleasing in all things, not answering back, not pilfering (*stealing*), but showing all good fidelity (*loyalty*), that they may adorn the doctrine of God our Savior in all things."

4. Can even sincere Christians be tempted to steal (pilfer) from their employers?
5. What should Christian employees do if they do their best, but their employers seems to be ungrateful or even take advantage of them?
6. How important is it to always be on time? What if you have a real good excuse for being late?
7. How does being a good employee adorn the doctrines of God and make the principles of the Bible appealing?

Be willing and learn to take responsibility. It may take time, but if you apply yourself in a responsible way, you will very likely have advantages and blessings for it in the long run. This is what Proverbs 22:29 is talking about: "Seest thou a man *diligent in his business*? He shall stand before kings; he shall not stand before mean (*or ordinary*) men." In other words, competent employees who apply themselves, though they may have to start at the very bottom, will usually progress to better circumstances, and most times, more compensation. A desire to be a competent employee, however, should be motivated by something nobler than a bigger paycheck or a higher position.

8. What main character trait makes one able to assume responsibility?
9. What is the basis of becoming a diligent and competent employee?

It is also important to accept responsibility for the mistakes that you make. An inability or unwillingness to do this is a hindrance in more ways than one. On the other hand, promptly and humbly admitting your mistakes and accepting responsibility for them usually builds good rapport, unless you keep repeating the same mistake.

10. What is the difference between being humble and being humiliated about your mistakes?

11. What does it mean to take responsibility for your mistakes?
12. Is making excuses ever in order? What about giving explanations?

In Luke 3:14, Jesus instructed His listeners to "Be content with your wages." Matthew 20:10-14 is another account about being satisfied with the paycheck. The kernel of the parable is, be thankful for the pay you agreed to, regardless of what others get. It happens today just like in Jesus' story: People might be quite satisfied with their pay scale, that is, until they find out someone else is getting more.

It should always be the desire of all people, especially Christians, to earn their paycheck. Do a day's work for a day's pay, even and especially when your boss is not looking or not present. After all, your employer cannot pull funds out of the sky to pay you; your efforts must generate the revenue for your pay.

A man named George had a reputation as an employee that coincided with his Christian profession. His boss said, "I can send George out to the woods all by himself, all day long, and when I come back in the evening, I can just count on it that George will have done a day's work for his day's pay. I really like George."

13. Colossians 4:1 says that masters shall pay what is *just and equal.* Does that give employees the right to make demands for what *they think* they deserve?
14. When people think they are being underpaid, do they ever have the right to perform less, according to the pay?
15. Employees, do you stay busy all day, even if you are unsupervised?

Practice good workmanship, and turn out sufficient volume of good quality product or performance. Stay busy, even when your boss is not watching. Go beyond "eye service." "Servants, obey in all things your masters according to the flesh; not with eyeservice, as menpleasers; but in singleness of heart, fearing God:" (Col. 3:22).

16. Does a proper fear of God always make people better and more productive employees?
17. How would you describe *men pleasers*?

Make it your goal to be a desirable employee, like Daniel was. "Then this Daniel was preferred above the presidents and princes, because an excellent spirit was in him" (Dan. 6:3).

18. Is "an excellent spirit" only and all about attitude, or are there other issues involved?
19. If one can't seem to have a good attitude or find joy in their job, should they quit?

Employees, be careful not to treat your boss as your equal. After all, he is your employer or your boss for a reason, and he has his responsibility to fulfill. First Timothy 6:1 says, "Let as many bondservants as are under the yoke count their own masters worthy of all honor, so that the name of God and His doctrine may not be blasphemed."

20. What does this have to do with blasphemy?

Be especially respectful to your boss if he is your brother (or sister) in the faith. This should make things work better, not worse. I Timothy 6:2 says, "And those who have believing masters, let them not despise them because they are brethren, but rather serve them because those who are benefited are believers and beloved."

In Psalm 55:13 David wrote about his difficulty in accepting negative input from someone who was "*mine equal*."

21. Why is it that too often people have more problems working for, or with a close family member, or a fellow church member, than for Mr. Public?

A poster in a hardware store read;

Rule #1: *The boss is always the boss.*
Rule #2: *When the boss is wrong, refer to rule #1.*

Do you get the message? He is still the boss, even when he is in fact wrong. Don't try to boss your boss. Don't try to force your opinions or instructions on him. Remember, he is the boss. Allow him to retain his position.

22. But sometimes bosses really fail. What shall an employee finally do if the boss is actually and continually in the wrong?

If you need or want time off, first consider that needing and wanting is not necessarily the same thing. But, it is altogether proper and in order for your employer to expect you to ask for your desire. Do not just presumptuously or demandingly announce your intentions. From your viewpoint it may seem to be no problem, but it is not fair to your boss. Likely you have never been in his position. If you are unhappy with the boss's requirements, it might help if you at least try to see things from his point of view. Christian employees should be loyal to the one who is giving them a job.

23. If the required days or hours are continually undesirable, is it acceptable to say, "I quit"?
24. If it seems the boss never cheerfully lets you have time off, is it okay to gripe a bit?

Be thankful for your job and don't even think about striking. If thankfulness is a problem, imagine not having a job. There are many people in the world who don't. Right now there are probably many who would gladly take what a lot of North Americans are dissatisfied with. It could even be that your employer is not enthused about being an employer and is doing you a favor by giving you a job

25. Can anything be done to improve our gratitude for employment in general?
26. Can you quote any scriptures that apply to this issue?

Be careful of your attitude on the job. It is good to consider what effect a job atmosphere will have on you, but it is perhaps even more pertinent to think about what difference you will make in the job environment. You influence your co-workers and others, one way or another, either for good or bad. Examples have well demonstrated that a good attitude on the job can be an influence for good years into the future. Sometimes the good effects linger long after the person has left the job.

Although wages are an important factor, thinking of your job only as a money-earning chore will certainly hinder your Christian witness at work. A two-mile attitude is far superior to a give-me-because-I-want outlook. Obvious selfishness can totally void your claims of Christianity.

Even, or perhaps especially, on your job, *a merry heart does good like medicine* (Prov. 17:22) for you as well as your co-workers. Cheerfulness and acceptance of job conditions and requirements can be an exceptionally effective witness for the Lord.

27. How does 2 Timothy 2:3 apply to challenging job circumstances?
28. If a person becomes aware that his attitude on the job has not been good, should he quietly change, or should he make an apology and state his new intentions?
29. What direction or encouragement would you give to a young person who faces ridicule on the job because of his effort to live up to Bible principles?

Self-Employment
CHAPTER 10

Being self-employed is not for everyone. God has not made all people alike. Some are well suited to be self-occupied, and some are not. In the eyes of God and in the minds of humble Christians, neither one is above the other. There is a place for those with talents to be self-employed. There is also a need for employers to supply jobs for those who are better suited to be employees.

1. Why do many people think it is lowly not to be self-employed?
2. How can people know what they are best suited for?

If you want to become self-employed, give careful thought to your reasons and motives. Erroneous aspirations can be a definite roadblock to success. Being self-employed requires lots of self-discipline and includes a lot of responsibility. Among other things you have to learn that cash on hand, or cash flow, is not the same as spendable profit. To be successful you must be governed by common sense and the rules of business, not by available money or credit. You will need to stay straight even when no one is looking over your shoulder.

3. Can anyone who really wants to, learn the necessary character qualities for being self-employed?
4. What are proper reasons for desiring to be self-employed?

If you are, or will be self-employed, you become responsible to manage your income tax liabilities. No one will withhold and deposit your taxes. You must see to it that proper records are kept, all the necessary forms are filed, and tax estimates are paid on time. This is a problem for many people. It takes planning and self-discipline, and for many people, it may require the help of an accountant. For farmers the requirements are somewhat different than for businesses; however, they require the same discipline. Irresponsibility in these areas results in costly penalties and a breach in integrity.

5. Is it ever acceptable for a Christian to voluntarily default and pay the penalty?

Whatever you do, whether you are employed by another, or self-employed, do it heartily as unto the Lord in spirit and attitude (Col. 3:23). This will help to make daily life more meaningful and more worth living.

6. What does it really mean to put your heart into your work, as unto the Lord?

Much good is to be said for work and for being gainfully occupied; however, remember to take a day off at the beginning of every week. This is not the Sabbath Day as in the Old Testament, but a New Testament practice initiated immediately after the time of Christ. It is very good to maintain the voluntary ethic of Sunday for a day of rest and worship, as practiced by the early Christian church.

8. How much or what type of labor is acceptable for Sunday?
9. By what rule do you decide?
10. What degree of emergency supersedes normal practice?

Thankfulness, Gratitude and Contentment

CHAPTER 11

There appears to be a certain temporal happiness and sense of accomplishment that people experience when they find success in natural things and acquire property. These sentiments are generally okay, but they are fleeting and often disappointing if that's where we look for happiness and fulfillment. Total fulfillment and satisfaction on the earth does not seem to be in God's plan for us.

Honest and sincere Christians, however, can possess sentiments of joy, peace and contentment that have nothing to do with money, material goods or ease of life. Christians should have a foundation of thankfulness and fulfillment that is not based on earthly things and circumstances.

1. How would you explain the foundation of real and enduring contentment and thankfulness?
2. Can any earthly thing in any way enhance real contentment and happiness?

Luke 17:12-19 speaks about that one man out of ten who returned to Jesus to express his thankfulness and gratitude for his healing. One would think they would all have wanted to thank the great physician. But ninety percent of those who were cleansed failed to glorify God and to give thanks.

3. Are the statistics any better today?
4. Could it be that today Jesus would ask, didn't I specifically bless 10,000 of my people; where are the 9000?
5. Is unexpressed thankfulness of any value? If so, in what way?

This is another subject that lays responsibility on parents to train children by teaching and example, so they will grow up to be thankful adults. Being a personal example, of course, will have the most positive effects. However, little custom-made lessons can leave lasting and powerful impressions that will foster ongoing thankfulness.

6. Is it possible to be too effusive with expressions and thereby cheapen the effect of verbal thanksgiving?
7. In the normal course of life, how can parents remember to give their children spontaneous lessons in this and other virtues?

It seems that abundant blessings can dull the human mind. Read Deuteronomy 8:7-11. The kernel of the message is, when things go well, "beware lest you forget the Lord."

An elderly gentleman shared some of his experiences about growing up as a child during the Great Depression in the 1930s. He said that his mother reserved certain foods always and only for specified holidays, birthdays, or other special occasions. No matter how hard they begged, those foods were strictly reserved for their special days or occasions. Therefore, he said, when those special days came around, that meal was precious. Then he lamented that these days people eat whatever they like until they are sick of it. Then they go for something new and indulge in that until they are tired of it, and nothing seems to be precious or thankworthy anymore.

In the United States, Canada, and a few other countries, people have had it so good for so long that they appear to think this is normal and that they deserve it this way. There seems to be a diminishing amount of true gratitude and thankfulness.

A formerly blind lady was shopping in a grocery store when she heard people complaining about the increasing food prices. Because of her experience with blindness, she said she felt like shouting at them, but aren't you glad you can see! Unfortunately there are frequent cases of people complaining, sometimes even bitterly, *with their mouths full.*

At the other end of the spectrum are people very grateful for things and circumstances that others would consider absolutely despicable. A group of Christians were fleeing for their lives due to persecution for their faith. They became so desperately destitute, that when they came upon an infestation of rats, they were very thankful for a source of meat. Proverbs 27:7 speaks about this very thing: "The full soul loatheth an honeycomb; but to the hungry soul every bitter thing is sweet."

8. What have you to say about the elderly gentleman's observations?
9. Why is it that people seem more thankful when they have less?
10. And why do we so easily forget, when the going is good?
11. Can these faults be corrected without experiencing hardship?

1 Thessalonians 5:18 gives this injunction: "In everything give thanks: for this is the will of God." Really? In everything? It may not mean that we shall be thankful for everything that occurs, but thankful regardless of whatever happens. It will do us good to consider Habakkuk 3:17-18, for an example of a grateful attitude *in everything*. "Although the fig tree shall not blossom, neither shall fruit be in the vines; the labour of the olive shall fail, and the fields shall yield no meat; the flock shall be cut off from the fold, and there shall be no herd in the stalls: Yet I will rejoice in the Lord, I will joy in the God of my salvation."

12. Does this type of gratitude require a divine infilling?

The privilege and ability to enjoy the good of our labors is a gift from God. See Ecclesiastes 2:24 and 5:19. This realization should go hand in hand with thankfulness and gratitude and have a positive impact on how we use our abilities and substance.

13. Are we guilty of ingratitude if we take for granted the privilege to enjoy a good meal as a result of applying ourselves to our work?

Proverbs 3:9-10 says that honoring the Lord with one's substance has the promise of full barns.

14. Is this way of honoring the Lord a part of expressing gratitude? How do we do it?
15. Does this connect with Jesus' teachings about the use of our talents?

Don't forget to be genuinely thankful for favors, even small ones, granted to you by another, whether he is a close friend, a neighbor, or a stranger. Perhaps someone lent you a tool, someone gave you an interest-free loan, someone helped you in a time of trouble, someone gave you a gift or a lift, or someone took time to give you a listening ear. If you are a renter, be grateful to your landlord for his housing provision for you and pay your rent cheerfully with thanksgiving. If you have a decent job, be grateful to your employer. One could make a long list about a host of other things.

16. Is this some of what it means about being thankful *in everything*?
17. What can you do about it if you tend to just forget?

In the Scripture we find that contentment is a command: "and be content with such things as you have." Hebrews 13:5. Here it appears that contentment is a matter of one's choice. First Timothy 6:6, 7 says that "godliness *with contentment* is great gain. (Some translations say *great wealth* in place of *great gain.*) For we brought nothing into this world, and it is certain we can carry nothing out."

18. Can you explain the process of choosing to be content?
19. What is the *great gain* that is to be attained by godliness with contentment?

Genuine contentment conserves mental strength and frees the mind for constructive living in the Lord's blessing. Discontentment and fretting have a burdensome effect on one's life and become a hindrance in mind and body.

True contentment makes it possible to be satisfied with *less than the best and less than the rest.* It should also make one satisfied with more than others (if so be your lot in life) and with the increased responsibilities that come with that lot in life. This has to do with an acceptance of ourselves and being willing to be what God made us to be. We should concentrate on redeeming our lot in life, without doing a lot of comparing with others.

20. What is the value of being satisfied with less than the best?
21. May a person then never wish for different or better circumstances?

Do not let yourself get unduly dissatisfied with your things (cars, clothing, furniture, equipment, etc.), that still fill the need well. Our thinking can play tricks on us, and we become erroneously convinced that we of necessity have to update or make a change. This can also be the fruit of a general restlessness. Sometimes people wrongly conclude that without question, they deserve and are entitled to their wishes. Frequently making changes for something new, or just different, or hopefully better, is usually costly and generally does not make people more satisfied or content. True contentment and fulfillment cannot be attained by acquiring possessions, even though they can bring temporary good feelings. Solomon spoke about his experience with this issue in Ecclesiastes 2:4-11, where he wrote, in short, I got me whatever I wanted, but it was a vain pursuit.

On a slightly different note, often people will be content and thankful with their lot in life, until they see others who seem to have a better fortune, or appear to have gotten a better deal or a more desirable item. Consider those wage earners in Matthew 20:9-11, who had gladly agreed to a certain wage, but then became very discontent when others were paid the same wage for less work.

22. How can a person keep from becoming generally dissatisfied with their things or their lot in life?
23. Is it ever acceptable to become dissatisfied because others excel over you or get a better business deal or a more desirable house, etc?

We are living in a time that, we might say, is an enemy to these virtues. The continual and fast pace of change, all the affluence and the abundant choice of things set the stage for dissatisfaction. It is said that the speed and volume of changes make people insecure, discontent and unthankful.

24. Is this how it really is?
25. Would it help to live more separated, or even withdrawn, from general society?

Thankfulness and contentment do not occur naturally nor inadvertently, neither for the rich nor for the poor. But there are some practical things one can do to learn realistic contentment and thankfulness and to actually attain to 1 Timothy 6:8: "And having food and raiment let us be therewith content." The apostle Paul wrote that he had learned the secret, "in any state to be content" (Phil. 4:11-13).

Following is a short list of things that should be a help to gain and strengthen these qualities:

- Accepting one's lot in life, willingly and cheerfully
- Accepting oneself, (See Romans 9:20-21. Why hast thou made me thus?)
- Learning to utilize and to enjoy what you already have
- Thinking seriously about being without the things you presently have
- Letting go of desires for what is beyond your reach or control
- Counting your many blessings; and really, most North Americans do have many
- Always looking beyond the things and circumstances of life to eternal things

This is only a small list of suggestions, so open your mind to God and the Scriptures for direction for yourself.

26. To some degree, because of the great variety in life's circumstances, every person has to find their own place of contentment. True or false?

True gratitude, coupled with contentment, is a great quality. It is an antidote for selfishness and a lack of concern for others. It should make you a willing giver and ready helper. It should end or at least greatly curtail complaining, envy and jealousy, etc, and provide for a smoother life. Real contentment is not dependent on possessions, circumstances, social standing, or treatment from other people. It is a quality from within. Having a little with the fear of the Lord is much better than having much, amid trouble and hatred. See Proverbs 15:16-17. And remember, the best things in life are free.

27. How can people help each other to attain this great quality of true gratitude?

There might be people who are content when they shouldn't be. For instance, some might be content just looking out for themselves, their family and their own interests, when the Lord would want them to look away, beyond their own surroundings, to other people and things. Consider Abram of old: he might have said, no, this is good enough; I'll just stay here and enjoy myself with my place and my things. God had other plans for him. So it might be today for numerous ones if they would be open to the Lord. Some might be asked to go, and others will be expected to stay and "bloom where they are planted."

28. How can one determine whether they might have a specific calling?
29. Does the Lord not allow us to choose our course in life?
30. What safety measures are there to keep people from getting carried away with their own thinking on this subject?

FINDING FULFILLMENT

Following are a few of many scriptures that relate to experiencing fulfillment as you make your way through life.

"Oh that men would praise the Lord for his goodness, and for his wonderful works to the children of men! For he satisfieth the longing soul, and filleth the hungry soul with goodness" (Ps. 107: 8-9).

"Nevertheless he left not himself without witness, in that he did good, and gave us rain from heaven, and fruitful seasons, filling our hearts with food and gladness" (Acts 14:17).

"Now no chastening for the present seemeth to be joyous, but grievous: *nevertheless afterward it yieldeth the peaceable fruit of righteousness* unto them which are exercised thereby. Wherefore lift up the hands which hang down, and the feeble knees; And make straight paths for your feet . . . Follow peace with all men, and holiness, without which no man shall see the Lord" (Heb. 12:11-14).

1. Is it acceptable for a person to feel at least a little self-satisfied about their accomplishments or circumstances in life?
2. If so, in what way? If not, what may they feel?
3. Can you share any real-life illustrations of the scriptural sense of fulfillment?

Giving and Other Benevolent Deeds

CHAPTER 12

This is a very important subject. Giving is a very prominent Bible teaching with far reaching implications. Learning to be a giver and a helper is vital because it's the right thing to do, and because being a generous person normally has a very positive effect on one's life. Normally there are benefits for the giver and the receiver. Among other valuable points is that giving helps to defeat greed. It appears that even a non-Christian will often reap good benefits for being a giving person.

Due to the selfish nature of all humanity it is easy to make the erroneous conclusion that whatever comes my way, is all mine. Remember, everything really belongs to God. Selfishness and unwillingness to give and to share will generally hinder the flow of blessings from God. This point is plainly explained in 2 Corinthians 9:6 where it says, "He who sows sparingly will also reap sparingly, and he who sows bountifully will also reap bountifully."

In the Old Testament tithing was a clear mandate. (See Deuteronomy 14:22-23.) Furthermore, God requested the first fruit and the best of the flock. (See Leviticus 23:10-12.) This might be interpreted to mean that God did not want blemished offerings or leftovers.

1. Can you explain the Old Testament meaning of tithing?
2. Does the tithing principle carry over into the New Testament?
3. Is giving to people in need the same as giving to the Lord?
4. If so, on what do you base your conclusion?
5. Is there any commendation in willingness to give away a used item, after acquiring a new one?

6. Should one perhaps sometimes give the new one to the person in need?

A proper attitude about giving and other generosities is very important. It is expedient to be a giver from the heart. Don't give grudgingly or of necessity, but willingly and cheerfully. Second Corinthians 9:7 has a promise of obtaining God's favor for giving with a proper attitude: "Every man according as he purposeth in his heart, *so let him give*; not grudgingly, or of necessity: for God loveth a cheerful giver."

Being a cheerful giver should become easier if we keep in mind that "The earth is the Lord's, and the fullness thereof; the world, and they that dwell therein" (Ps. 24:1). Whatever we give, we are but giving what is already His anyway. Song writer John Whittier (1807-1892) wrote about this in his hymn, "All Things are Thine": "Thine own before thy feet we lay." In addition Acts 20:35 tells us that "It is more blessed to give than to receive."

7. Based on these thoughts, can *anyone* find joy in being a giver?
8. How will this joy be felt, or what is its effect?

Luke 6:38 has more to say about the results of upbeat giving: "Give, and it shall be given unto you; good measure, pressed down, and shaken together, and running over, shall men give into your bosom. For with the same measure that ye mete withal it shall be measured to you again."

9. Is coerced giving better than not giving at all?
10. Does generosity always pay big dividends?
11. Can a person ever give too much?
12. What are some things deacons could do to encourage giving in their congregations?

SHARING AND HELPING

The true spirit of giving and sharing, however, goes far beyond putting money in an offering basket. It also includes our time, talent, love, helping hands, willingness to share, lending to those in need, and even simply giving a listening ear to someone in a struggle. James 1:27 talks about giving of your time to "visit the fatherless and the widows." And if you are sensitive to the Holy Spirit, you might include a gift for tangible necessities.

For some people, true giving might also include willingness to serve as a missionary, or some other forms of service. There seems to be a constant need for helpers for a wide range of needs. The Good Samaritan from Luke 10:33-37 is a good example of a "Johnny-on-the-spot" giver. He saw a need, and then and there he did what he could.

1. What is required for a person to become a willing, benevolent giver?
2. Under what conditions might it be unwise to be a Good Samaritan?
3. Can it ever happen that a person might rightfully regret having given or helped?
4. Can one know if and when giving or helping would have a negative end result?
5. Can you give an example of how this could happen?

Do not excuse yourself from giving because you are not rich. Consider the poor widow who gave her last two mites and the widow who had only a little meal and oil but first baked a cake for the prophet. It appears people in general are more willing to give when they have less and more disposed to share in hard times than in good times.

6. What causes this paradox in human behavior?

Affluent times appear to create an independent attitude about giving and accepting help. When economic conditions are such that people have less, they need each other more, and seem to be more willing to help and be helped. When economic conditions are better, to the point of affluence, it seems that people are expected to take care of themselves.

7. Is this fact scripturally okay?
8. If not, what should be done about it?

Although giving has the promise of blessings in many scriptures, in real life, giving does not always pay off in the form of a quick, or even an eventual, return in the time of our life. There are times when giving (money, mind or muscle) requires willingness to give at your own expense. We do not read that the Good Samaritan was compensated in any way for his expense and kindness to the unfortunate man along the way. Sometimes you may wonder if giving or helping was the right thing to do in a given situation. Someone may even think you were foolish. God alone, however, retains the right to judge the matter and the outcome.

9. Should we therefore do our charitable deeds and never look back?
10. Is this another one of the places where "God moves in a mysterious way"?

In Luke 18:28 Peter made a statement about sacrificial living. He told Jesus, "Lo, we have left all, and followed thee."

11. What did Jesus answer Peter?

Proverbs 11:24 says, "There is that scattereth, and yet increaseth; and there is that withholdeth more than is meet, but it tendeth to poverty." It has been said that this is possibly the oldest paradox in the world. One gives generously, here and there, yet his assets increase. Another keeps more than he needs, but it seems to make him poor.

The widow's experience in 1 Kings, chapter 17, serves as an example of this. When she had only a little meal and oil left, Elijah the prophet asked her to "make me thereof a little cake first." By giving what she thought was her last substance, she and her son were miraculously blessed with ongoing provisions.

12. How can Proverb 11:24 be true?
13. Can you give any current-day illustrations of an apparent increase by giving?

When people are committed to be givers, there might be a few that actually give too much, but generally they are very few.

14. Why?
15. What might constitute over-giving?
16. Do you know of any cases of this happening?

It has been said that real charity is not dependent on a tax deduction. Although a tax deduction is entirely legal and in order within the rules; there are perhaps many places when the Lord might want to inspire you to give when you cannot claim a tax deduction.

17. Is it ever right to hesitate when you know you can't claim a deduction?

Because of our humanness, we need to watch lest our possessions become so precious that we can't bring ourselves to be willing givers. Don't be selfish; give God His share. Consider God's challenge in Malachi 3:8-10. In essence God told them, just try me; give me a chance. Do your giving and see "*if I will not open you the windows of heaven, and pour you out a blessing, that there shall not be room enough to receive it.*"

18. Some say that if we don't give God his share, He takes it. Is that true?
19. What would be a current-day explanation of *the windows of heaven being opened* if we meet the conditions?
20. In what forms might blessings come because of giving?

Giving to right causes is not similar to throwing money away; it's more like purchasing a blessing. In Malachi 3:11, God promised to "rebuke the devourer . . . neither shall your vine cast her fruit before the time."

21. Does this principle apply today?
22. Can God rebuke mechanical failure, for example, as well as fruit bugs and other pests?

Though giving is important, be careful about trying to "buy yourself rich" by giving (a little or a lot), but rather give from a desire to serve God. Furthermore, you can't buy righteousness by giving in *any* amount. Even if you give away everything you have, it will do you no good if your motive or attitude is wrong. The Apostle Paul said, "And though I bestow all my goods to feed the poor, and though I give my body to be burned, and have not charity, it profiteth me nothing" (1 Corinthians13:3).

Most healthy people are sooner or later called upon for service of some kind. Take your calling or assignment seriously. Give yourself and serve diligently, at home, in the church, on the job, wherever or whatever it is.

You may think of many reasons why it doesn't seem to be the right time, or that you're not the right person, or your circumstances don't allow it, or your family won't agree, etc. We read about this in Haggai 1:2-6. "This people say, The time is not come, the time that the Lord's house should be built. Then came the word of the Lord by Haggai the prophet, saying, Is it time for you, O ye, to dwell in your ceiled houses, and this house lie waste? Now therefore thus saith the Lord of hosts; Consider your ways. Ye have sown much, and bring in little; ye eat, but ye have not enough; ye drink, but ye are not filled with drink; ye clothe you, but there is none warm; and he that earneth wages earneth wages to put it into a bag with holes."

In the era this was written, it must have been a luxury to have a ceiling in one's house. Further, the people were apparently excusing themselves from helping to rebuild the temple of God and were rather making their own houses nice and luxurious.

In the New Testament era this surely applies to building or working in the spiritual house of God, as well as other ways. This scripture and others imply that we must be careful about being so caught up in our own affairs that we excuse ourselves from helping others, or giving ourselves to personal or spiritual needs or causes.

23. Are many people hurting, struggling, or suffering because too many Christians are occupied with, putting "ceilings in their own houses" or acquiring and arranging current-day luxuries and nice things?
24. How would you explain the verse in Haggai 2:1-6 about sowing much and reaping little, etc? Does it happen yet today?

Jesus said that the opportunity to help the poor will always be here. "For ye have the poor with you always, and whensoever ye will ye may do them good" (Mark 14:7).

25. Who are they today?
26. Why are they poor?

27. What shall we do when their circumstances appear to be their fault?

Concerning helping the poor, James 2:16 says to not only wish them well, but do something if you can. Blessings are promised to those who are willing to help the poor and the needy. "Blessed is he that considereth the poor: the Lord will deliver him in time of trouble. The Lord will preserve him, and keep him alive; and he shall be blessed upon the earth: and thou wilt not deliver him unto the will of his enemies" (Ps. 41:1-2). "Blessed are the merciful: for they shall obtain mercy" (Matt.5:7). "He that hath a bountiful eye shall be blessed; for he giveth of his bread to the poor"(Prov. 22:9). And there are more.

28. Can you spot the promised blessing in each of the above scriptures?
29. There are right ways and wrong ways to help the poor; how can one know the difference?

In these affluent times, the volume and types of gifts given at big weddings might be beyond what is really a blessing for the young couple in the long run.

30. Is there reason for concern about this?
31. If so, what can or should be done about it?

With the proper attitude and motive, church aid plans, sharing plans and other charity organizations are an excellent opportunity for sharing. However if we are only interested in our own protection or advantage, we will likely lose the blessings of being a giver, even to such honorable organizations.

32. What is the proper attitude for participating in church-sponsored aid plans?

Look beyond your own things and interests and be willing to serve others, perhaps your neighbor in need, possibly through some charity work, maybe in a volunteer program, or perhaps even as a missionary. Or the Lord may inspire you to do some good deed, even though no one may ever realize it. Perhaps even the very recipient might never be aware of it. But remember, God sees in secret. As you go out to do good deeds, keep one thing in mind, though, that real charity starts at home!

33. What is the secret for sincere and spontaneous charitable serving?
34. How hard should we strive to stay anonymous when doing good for others?

Another form of giving is to help others with a loan. Jesus taught that we shall be willing to give and lend to those in need, even if we might never get it back. "Give to him that asketh thee, and from him that would borrow of thee turn not thou away" (Matt. 5:42). "And if ye lend to them of whom ye hope to receive, what thank have ye? for sinners also lend to sinners, to receive as much again. But love ye your enemies, and do good, and lend, hoping for nothing again; and your reward shall be great, and ye shall be the children of the Highest: for he is kind unto the unthankful and to the evil. Be ye therefore merciful, as your Father also is merciful" (Luke 6:34-36).

Proverbs 19:17 says, "He that hath pity upon the poor lendeth unto the Lord; and that which he hath given will he pay him again." This coincides with Matthew 25:40: "Inasmuch as ye have done it unto one of the least of these my brethren, ye have done it unto me."

35. What vision or understanding will make people more ready to lend or give to the poor?
36. Are we supposed to not even *hope* to be repaid?
37. Do all poor people deserve a loan or a lift?
38. For people who have received a helping loan, does the scripture from Luke 6, referred to above, give them any right not to repay it?

Deuteronomy 15:7-11 cautions about being unwilling help a poor man because of the Law's provision to forgive debts every seventh year. "If there be among you a poor man of one of thy brethren within any of thy gates in thy land which the Lord thy God giveth thee, thou shalt not harden thine heart, nor shut thine hand from thy poor brother: But thou shalt open thine hand wide unto him, and shalt surely lend him sufficient for his need, *in that* which he wanteth. Beware that there be not a thought in thy wicked heart, saying, The seventh year, the year of release, is at hand; and thine eye be evil against thy poor brother, and thou givest him nought; and he cry unto the Lord against thee, and it be sin unto thee. Thou shalt surely give him, and thine heart shall not be grieved when thou givest unto him: because that for this thing the Lord thy God shall bless thee in all thy works, and in all that thou puttest thine hand unto. For the poor shall never cease out of the land: therefore I command thee, saying, Thou shalt open thine hand wide unto thy brother, to thy poor, and to thy needy, in thy land."

39. How might this apply to us today?

By being willing, or even eager, to give someone in need a lift, you can earn a treasure much more valuable than interest or profits from any prospective investments. Psalm 15:1 and 5, simply put, talk about the privilege to dwell in God's holy hill and have the blessing of God on your efforts in life.

40. Can you name any other scriptures that apply to this subject?

Youth and even children are not exempt from the possibility or responsibility to help others who are unfortunate or otherwise in need. It's a good idea for all Christian youth, if practical, to give time to some type of voluntary service. There are many different ways to do this. This should help to set a valuable pattern of unselfish, charitable living.

41. In what way are parents responsible to help or influence children to accomplish this?

Surveys have shown that for most people, the best and most opportune time to make useful contributions to society (and to the Lord) seems to be during their fifties. Normally by this time they have gained valuable experience and usually are in a financial position to be of useful service. Although no age group is exempt, perhaps you should make a special attempt to make your "fifties" contribution to society in a good way. Ultimately though, everyone should try to contribute more to life and society than he takes.

42. What can be done if tomorrow always seems to be a better time to give than today?
43. What do you think it means to give more than you take during your time on the earth?

Finally, here follows a word of encouragement to deacons (and future deacons). A faithful, willing deacon who is diligent and careful in his work and bookkeeping for the church, as well as in his own personal life and occupation, will be an unconscious impetus to make people feel like being cheerful givers. This principle is not limited to deacons; it applies to many people in many ways. Collectively, a church congregation should be willing to give far and wide, because of love, and to rise above possible congregational selfishness.

Though we cannot mandate what the Lord shall do for us because we have been a giver, yet let us give Him a chance to bless us as He sees fit, by being willing, cheerful givers.

HOSPITALITY

Do not neglect to give hospitality. This subject might immediately give us thoughts of entertaining company in our homes. But true Christian hospitality is much more than having company for a meal or for the night. Titus 1:8 says, "But a lover of hospitality, a lover of good men, sober, just, holy, temperate." Also Romans 12:10 and 13 says, "Be kindly affectioned one to another with brotherly love; in honour preferring one another; Distributing to the necessity of saints; given to hospitality."

It has been said that real hospitality begins when we are willing to fill a need even though it is inconvenient or undesirable. Self-centeredness will keep us from giving this type of real hospitality.

1. How would you explain true Christian hospitality?
2. Give some examples of hospitality that goes beyond the aspect of meals and lodging.

Hebrews 13:1-2 gives another command and reason for being hospitable: "Let brotherly love continue. Be not forgetful to entertain strangers: for thereby some have entertained angels unawares."

3. What effect should this scripture have on our hospitality?
4. Will some people have been hospitable to angels and never known it or even given it a thought?
5. Should Christian people be free to invite friend and stranger alike?

How mindful should one be about the cost of hosting visitors or inviting meal guests? Some people may throw caution to the wind to make a good impression with the quality and quantity of provisions and preparations. Others may be tempted to be self-centered and unwilling to "spend and be spent" to do good deeds like the Good Samaritan.

6. Should Christians ever consider the cost of entertaining company?
7. Is it right to spend and do more for company than for your family?

Between being too lavish and being too tight, there is a way to humbly and honestly reach out and do good to our fellow people, even to those who are unable to repay us. "But when thou makest a feast, call the poor, the maimed, the lame, the blind: And thou shalt be blessed; for they cannot recompense thee: for thou shalt be recompensed at the resurrection of the just" (Luke 14:13-14).

8. What do you make of this scripture?
9. Can you give an explanation of a realistic, present-day application of this teaching?

Romans 12:13 talks about "Distributing to the necessity of saints; given to hospitality."

Today (and tomorrow) see how much good you can do, not how little you can get by with.

Be careful though, about giving or doing good "to be seen of men" or to make self-promoting impressions. Matthew 6:1-4 cautions about this when it says we should not sound a trumpet, but rather do it in secret, and let God, who sees in secret, reward you as He sees fit.

10. What kind of rewards do you expect to receive?

Following is a writing found in a motel room that relates to hospitality.

TO OUR GUESTS

In ancient times there was a prayer "for the stranger within our gates."

Because this motel is a human institution to serve people and not solely a money-making organization, we hope that God will grant you peace and rest while you are under our roof.

May this room and motel be your "second" home. May those you love be near to you in thoughts and dreams. Even though we may not get to know you, we hope that you will be as comfortable and happy as if you were in your own home.

May the business that brought you our way prosper. May every call you make and every message you receive add to your joy. When you leave, may your journey be safe.

We are all travelers. From birth till death we travel between eternities. May these days be pleasant for you, profitable for society, helpful for those you meet, and a joy to those who know and love you best.

Thank you,

Your gracious hosts. *Anonymous*

11. In what way would this apply to hosting overnight guests in one's home?

Savings and Investments

CHAPTER 13

There are several basic aspects to saving: one is to keep what you already have, and another is to avoid expenses by proper planning, careful management, and discipline. Although faith in God is the main matter to help us not to worry about tomorrow; yet saving a common sense cushion fund does help to eliminate anxiety and stress. It has been said that we should live by a "10-10-80" formula, meaning that we should give away 10 percent, save 10 percent, and live on the remaining 80 percent. Living by such a formula could make a big difference for the better in many people's lives.

1. Is the 10-10-80 formula scriptural?
2. Why is it so easy to spend and so hard to save for most people?

Saving by avoiding expenses or simply not spending applies in numerous ways. One is by taking forethought and finding ways to get by with what you have or sometimes spending a small amount to evade a larger expense. Another is to stick to your plan so you will not be influenced to buy when you shouldn't. Analysts say the longer the merchant can keep you in his store, the more you will buy. So a good practice would be to go in, buy what you need, and get out of the store. There are also other reasons not to loiter in stores and shopping malls.

3. Can you name more ways this type of discipline will save you money?
4. What other problems can be avoided by not lingering in shopping malls?

There are important reasons why everyone should learn to save, the sooner or younger the better. The discipline required to set aside funds for the future will have far-reaching and helpful effects in many areas of your life. Children can be taught to save with any gifts they receive. Wise youth will begin to save for their future as soon as they acquire or start earning money.

The following quote relates to reasons for learning to save. "*If you cannot save money, the seed of success is not in you*" (J. J. Hill).

5. How important is it to learn to save?
6. Is Mr. Hill's statement true?

Luke 14:28 refers to the discipline of laying aside for a purpose: "For which of you, intending to build a tower, sitteth not down first, and counteth the cost, whether he have sufficient to finish it?"

7. How does this relate to the teaching in Matthew 6:34, about taking no thought for the morrow?

"Upon the first day of the week let every one of you *lay by him in store*, as God hath prospered him, that there be no gatherings when I come" (1 Cor. 16:2). This verse speaks about saving (to lay by in store) for the sake of giving. It also implies varying amounts of saving and giving, *as God has prospered.* The more God prospers you, the more you should lay aside to give.

8. How would you explain the term; *lay by him in store*?
9. Should we concern ourselves with laying aside savings for our old age?

Being a saving person goes far beyond stockpiling money. It's a conservative and prudent way of life that tends to become natural with practice and exercise. However; for all the good that is to be said in favor of saving, there is a big difference between saving and selfish hoarding. Do you know the difference?

Even though saving is good, beware of becoming a miser, which means to live very meagerly because of an immoderate desire to hoard wealth. Ecclesiastes 5:13 says, "There is a sore evil which I have seen under the sun, namely, riches kept for the owners thereof to their hurt." This speaks about saving with such wrong motives or attitudes that in the end it becomes a hindrance to the saver and sometimes even to others. Verse 14 of the same chapter states that these savings are then often lost by "evil travail," or wrong business ventures and investments.

10. How would you explain the term *sore evil* used in this scripture?
11. Can you name some safety points to guard against this sore evil?

Proverbs 13:11 says, "He that gathereth by labour shall increase." This verse indicates that the person who applies himself will likely realize a gain in assets. Increase or accumulation is associated with work and the art of saving.

If you apply yourself in a properly functioning economy, sooner or later you will likely have more than enough for your basic needs. Then you will need to learn how not to buy or to do some things that you actually could afford. You might experience a strong desire or peer pressure to buy or to do certain things, yet Christian wisdom and common sense tells you it would be better not to. Some people, when they realize they have surplus funds, feel compelled to spend, and it may just slip through their fingers like sand.

12. What personal constitution is required to stay on course when a person has surplus funds?
13. Can you quote any scriptures that give direction for this issue?

One of the foremost and simplest ways to save is to stay at home and keep yourself gainfully occupied. When you do leave home, going visiting and fellowshipping instead of going out for recreational shopping or dining will save you lots of money. A penny saved is still a penny earned, even in the 21st century.

You must be on guard against the pressures that would influence you to spend your savings when you shouldn't. Many advertisements shout "Save!" but they really mean, come and spend! There are also cultural and peer pressures that can quickly take away your savings if you're not careful.

You can save much money by taking care of your things, using them with proper caution, and performing timely maintenance. Ecclesiastes

10:18 says, "Because of laziness the building decays, And through idleness of hands the house leaks." Slothfulness can in the end force you to spend your savings on costly repairs that could have been avoided.

Another basic way to avoid a lot of expense is by disciplining yourself to save first and then buy, instead of buying now and paying later, with interest. Savings of interest expense add up very fast if "first you save, and then you buy." With proper discipline and perseverance, large amounts can be saved, a little at a time, a little here and a little there, and sometimes more here and a lot there.

14. What can be done for the person who thinks that what little they are able to lay aside for savings is not worth the effort?
15. What does the old adage, *"A penny saved is a penny earned,"* mean?
16. The time before one gets married is the best time to build a saving fund. True or false?
17. To what degree are investments acceptable for Christians? What types are acceptable?
18. Is ownership of financial stock scripturally appropriate?

There might be many opinions about what to do with savings funds you are holding till it's time to use them. Seeking advice can be very helpful.

Here are a few suggestions for what to do with your savings:

A. Keep some readily available for a safety margin, for planned or imminent expenditures, for unexpected or emergency expenses, etc.
B. Make equity payments such as lease purchase of a house, or investment payments for a business or other self-employment opportunities, etc.
C. Lend it to someone in need.
D. Consider lending to church organizations that are serving the needs of people.
E. Lend to church-sponsored institutions, which can bring you a genuine blessing.
F. Lay it up in heaven by unselfish charitable contributions, or spending for charitable causes.
G. Become a part owner in shared real-estate ventures.

Here are also a few suggestions for where *not* to invest or to keep savings funds:

A. Where moth and rust can corrupt. See Matthew 6:20. This would include, but not be limited to stashes of currency, accumulations of collector's items, highly cherished heirlooms, costly antiques, guns, cars or anything that's highly esteemed and can rust or decay or be stolen.
B. Usury-bearing accounts or loans; according to Psalm 15:1 and 5, and other scriptures.
C. Adding land to land, and more land to yet more land, or any other inordinate and ever-increasing holdings.
D. Questionable, unethical or unsanctioned, for-profit ventures, or vain schemes, etc.

These are only a few suggestions. Open your mind to God's way for you, your family, and your circumstances.

19. Would it perhaps be better never to have any surplus?
20. Should one be concerned about devaluation of funds because of inflation?

Now let's switch to a totally different line of thought about saving. In Isaiah 24:5, we read about the earth being "defiled under the inhabitants thereof; because they have transgressed the laws." This seems to be talking about spoiling or wasting the earth's resources. An excellent article about this subject, "The Christian and the Environment," appeared in the *Messenger of Truth* (Sept. 13, 2000). A quote from the article states, "The moral code that our faith imposes upon us, forbids immoral and wasteful living." The concluding quote says, "The Christian ought to be an environmentalist in the truest sense."

21. What laws has God set in order that would apply to this subject?
22. What is happening today that relates to the scripture in Isaiah?
23. How much should Christians be concerned about environmental and conservation issues?
24. Name some ways that the quote about Christians being environmentalists should be true.
25. Should Christians be avid recyclers, etc?

After everything is said about savings issues, it is of utmost importance that you don't forget to establish your heavenly savings account and lay up treasures in heaven. "But lay up for yourselves treasures in heaven" (Matt. 6:20). There are many things that simply do not make sense to the earthly-minded person, but in the light of eternity they are very wise. A sincere Christian's attitude about earthly savings and investments may be one of those things.

26. What would you say is the main secret to finding God's will in this subject?
27. Is the scriptural ideal workable and attainable in this day and age?

Thrift

CHAPTER 14

Thrift is a good virtue that has much to do with balancing your finances. Unfortunately, because of a lack in personal restraint, thrift often goes out the door when good times come in. In practice, thrift is closely connected to personal restraint.

To a large extent, thrift refers to finding ways to avoid expenses. This applies in many ways. Being willing to make do with what you have can save lots of expenses. Often a small purchase and a willingness to do it yourself, can avoid a much larger expense.

Thrifty living also means not being wasteful, lavish or even just plain careless. Proverbs 12:27 speaks about carelessness: "The slothful man roasteth not that which he took in hunting: but the substance of a diligent man is precious." The hunter succeeds in getting something, but then he lets it go to waste. This applies in many things.

1. The better the economic circumstances the more the waste. Is that okay?
2. Why is someone who is a careless over-spender referred to as a spendthrift?

To be properly effective in your life, thrift should be learned before you are in a financial bind. On the other hand, a financial bind can force people to become more thrifty. With a little practice, thriftiness can become a natural way of life.

One example of up-front thrift is doing things to save energy: Flip the switch, re-adjust the thermostat, close the valve, shut the door, shorten the shower, stay at home. Such actions probably save more than you think.

3. Is a lack of thrift always extravagance, or is there a neutral place?
4. Do some folks not know how to be thrifty?

Jesus taught thriftiness with food, even when there was food to no end: "When they were filled, he said unto his disciples, Gather up the fragments that remain, that nothing be lost" (John 6:12). Another scripture that relates to food thrift is in Proverbs 21:20 says, "There is treasure to be desired and oil in the dwelling of the wise; but a foolish man spendeth it up." This verse implies that the wise person is thrifty and therefore has substance on hand. The thoughtless person carelessly or lavishly spends and uses everything, lives from hand to mouth and therefore can often be in need.

So, ladies, save the leftovers. Think twice before throwing it out.

4. Does God disapprove of living that's too liberal?
5. Does personal preference or choice justify one's level of living?

Affluence is a hindrance to the valuable lessons normally learned by *making do or doing without*. It also greatly lessens or weakens the learning experience when negligence and carelessness would otherwise force one to do without. Even in good times, the wise person will consider fixing something that doesn't work instead of thoughtlessly throwing it out and buying a new one.

Think twice before buying lots of single-use, disposable items. North Americans are very wasteful compared to much of the world.

An American lady who was in Africa over the Fourth of July attended a party with other Americans to celebrate Independence Day. "There at the party," she said, "I saw us and our practices through the eyes of the African people, and I was appalled at us."

It has been calculated that if the whole world were to live on the level of the people of the United States, five more planets would be required to sustain such living.

6. How should we feel about this, and what can we do about it?

Parents should teach their children, starting when they are young, to care for things in general: to be careful with their clothing, to take care of their toys, to return their bicycles and other things to their places. This goes a long way toward teaching thrift and good stewardship. Fathers can reinforce this by helping their children with maintenance and repair of their things.

A father saw his teenage daughter pitch her hairdryer into the trash and asked what was wrong with it. "It doesn't work," she said. "I'm going to have to get a new one." He took a look at it and found the air intake covered with lint. He cleaned it off, and the hairdryer worked as good as new.

7. Share your own thoughts of how parents should teach thrift.
8. Should parents sometimes mend something, though it might be more expedient to buy a new one, for the sake of teaching diligence and good stewardship?

The tenor of the Scriptures teaches that being conservative, thrifty and frugal is right. Being selfish, wasteful, stingy and miserly is not. Through the guidance of the Holy Spirit it should be possible to know the difference. Unfortunately, there is a tendency for people to think *they* have the right balance, and others around them seem to be over or under balanced.

9. Who is to say then, what is right? What is your guide?

Budgeting

CHAPTER 15

Budgeting also has a base in the Bible. "For which of you, intending to build a tower, sitteth not down first, and counteth the cost, whether he have sufficient to finish it? Lest haply, after he hath laid the foundation, and is not able to finish it, all that behold it begin to mock him, Saying, This man began to build, and was not able to finish" (Luke 14:28-30). "Who then is that faithful and wise steward (*who has control of things*), whom his lord shall make ruler over his household" (Luke 12:42).

Far too many people exist without a plan, financially and otherwise, and bump from one ultimatum to another. This is a result of the depraved human nature. The prodigal son was like that. He had no budget plan but simply spent lavishly and irrationally until it was all gone. It's much better to be a budgeter with a goal: Don't just spend it all.

There is more than one approach to this subject. The basics of budgeting are knowing your economic status, where you're headed financially, and whether your income and outgo will balance. It is creating an itemized summary of expected expenditures for a given period and a proposal to finance them. It is looking ahead and, with discipline, setting a plan in order to make things work.

Budgeting can be quite simple, but you must be realistic with your numbers, and you must stick with it. Take time to consider scriptural perspectives when planning a budget. A separate checking account to use only for scheduled payments and other specific expense can help to organize and manage your money. It can work as a safeguard to ensure that you will have the funds when the payments come due. Ideally, a budget plan should always show a margin of positive balance.

Basic steps to plan a budget:

A. Determine your revenue for a weekly, monthly or yearly period.
   1. Add up the income you expect from all sources. Be realistic.
   2. Add in usable assets and cash on hand to find your total usable funds.

B. Determine your probable expenditures for the same time period.
   1. Add up fixed expenses like house rent, mortgage payments, other monthly payments, taxes, etc.
   2. Add in other expected disbursements, including charitable donations.
   3. Consider including a savings amount for future expenses or emergencies.
   4. Add in an amount for a safety margin.

Now compare your usable income with your total expected expenses. Ideally the expected expenditures should always be less than, or at least not greater than, the usable income total. If it is greater, you must make adjustments, or you are headed for or already in trouble. If this is your case, you will find it is almost always easier to decrease your expenses than to increase your income. Start there to find your solution.

Suggested order of priorities for funds disbursements:

A. Charitable contributions
B. Savings for future plans and an emergency cushion, and to learn self-discipline
C. Fixed expenses such as house rent or mortgage payments, taxes, car payments, and other pre-set expenses
D. Regular monthly costs such as electricity, telephone, monthly allocation for real-estate taxes, etc.
E. Projected health-care and dental expenses
F. Discretionary expenses, such as food, clothing, travel, gifts and other flexible expenditures. (Discretionary refers to expenses that are, to a large extent, adjustable according to your judgment and discipline.)
G. Last on the list, if you think it's acceptable, expenses for unnecessary items and activities

Learning the prudence of spending less than you make will afford you a certain peace of mind about your finances. If you always spend less than you make, you will always have more than enough. Budgeting should help you to accomplish this.

Does that sound too simple?

Responsible Spending

CHAPTER 16

Your most valuable commodity for responsible spending is not money; it's your time. Though people do not have the same length of life, everyone has 24 hours a day. Don't just kill your time; redeem it, spend it wisely. "See then that ye walk circumspectly, not as fools, but as wise, Redeeming the time, because the days are evil" (Eph. 5:15-16). Christians should always endeavor to live productively and unselfishly. "So teach us to number our days, that we may apply our hearts unto wisdom" (Ps. 90:12).

1. People's ideas about how to use their time vary drastically. What are some pointers for how to spend your time so you can enjoy God's blessing on the days of your life?
2. What does it mean to *number our days*?
3. How much of their time should Christians spend for socializing?
4. Can adult game-playing be considered a wise use of time? If so, for what reasons, under what circumstances and how much?

To be a responsible user of your money and resources, you must have a budget plan or some way to control your spending. The willingness and fortitude to do this will normally bring you the blessing of an effective economic experience. On the other hand, if you don't control your spending, you will likely end up with many problems and hard struggles.

5. Is there a secret for finding joy in a lifestyle of controlled spending?
6. What can be done for those who would rather let loose and splurge, then suffer?

Since money is a tool for bartering, we could perhaps say that, after giving and saving, the remainder of your money is for spending. Few people appear to have a problem spending; it is responsible spending that is the challenge. This may be because most parents invest lots of time and funds teaching their children to earn money but very little time teaching them how to use it.

Most of the financial troubles people have are directly linked to undisciplined, uncalculated or uneducated spending. The prodigal son is a vivid Bible example of this. He was, as the word *prodigal* implies, wasteful, reckless and extravagant. In the end, he had to accept the consequences.

How you spend your money makes more of a difference than how much you have or how you get it. Often it is more feasible to fix a problem by controlling your spending, rather than trying to increase your earnings.

7. How can parents train their children to be wise spenders?
8. Must young people sometimes be allowed to waste some of their earnings so they can learn from their misjudgments and mistakes?
9. Do you agree that it is easier to remedy financial trouble by decreasing your spending than increasing your income?

UNDERSTANDING PRIORITIES

Priorities ordered according to common sense and spiritual relevance serves as a foundation of responsible spending. Sometimes people spend so much on extras that they cannot manage to pay for necessities, either not on time or not at all. Be careful about spending your money for "*that which is not bread and your labour for that which satisfieth not* (or for that which has no necessary purpose in life)" (Isa. 55:2). Many people get into trouble because they place luxuries and personal wants ahead of necessities. If you are confused about this issue, invite someone in whom you have confidence to assist you in sorting things out.

Following is a very basic three-point order of priorities:

- Actual needs always belong first on the list: clothing, food, shelter, heat and light.

- Next are those important but not absolute necessities like household items and furniture, transportation, communication equipment, hospitality facilities, etc.
- Last, is discretionary spending for optional items and activities.

10. Share your corrections or additions to this order of priorities.
11. In which category does health care belong?
12. Do you have any idea what percentage of your spending qualifies as necessary purchases?

SPENDING WITH WISDOM AND CONTROL

At times you may conclude that a certain item is right for you to buy. The fact that you have enough money in hand or in your checking account, or enough credit on your card does not mean you can afford to buy it. The same can be true about places you wish to go or things you would like to do.

1. How can this be true when, in fact, you have the means to buy right with you?
2. Might it be a case of "robbing Peter to pay Paul"? Do you know what that means?

A number of axioms blame wives of effortlessly spending money faster than their husbands can earn it.

3. Is this true?
4. If so, what about their daughters?

Statistics show that women in North America are, in fact, more inclined than a man to spend when they shouldn't. Men, however, are not exempt. It's said a man will restrain himself for a time, but then he will spend a larger amount on a whim and almost catch up with his wife. Perhaps there is some reason for the blame on women, but men are not excused.

5. How then can the husband safely trust his wife, and vice versa?

Try to always get at least "two birds with one stone." For example, aim to accomplish two or more purposes with one shopping trip. Make your moves count. Don't go to town every time you need one little thing. Find a way to do without and wait until you will be going for other reasons also. This principle applies in many ways. If you practice it, you will get positive results.

6. Share your thoughts or experiences about the above issue.

Avoid buying yourself into an expensive lifestyle. This happens when you buy things that force you to spend yet more. For example, if you buy a large, expensive, upscale house you will need to pay more real-estate taxes, buy more heat, spend more for up-keep and maintenance, etc. The same principle applies to many issues and can have a rapid domino effect that can break your finances.

7. What does it take to avoid this pitfall?
8. When this has happened, how can it be fixed?
9. Would a conscious objective of modesty, simplicity and economy help?

Manufacturers and retailers cater to the vanities of the human race. That is one reason why they continually introduce new models and new styles. They have learned what to make and how to market it, so it appeals to people's psychological makeup. This is especially true about things and activities that are not necessities in life.

10. What is the Christian's guard against these outside pressures to buy what he should not?

Depending on your needs and circumstances, buying the best and most expensive item available may be cheapest in the long run. Other times the cheapest can be the best buy because it may serve the purpose just as well as an expensive one. Or maybe that is all you can realistically afford.

11. Can you give an example of this?

In defense of buying superior quality products, an anonymous quote says, "*The bitter taste of poor quality lingers long after the sweetness of low price is forgotten.*" This may often be true.

12. How then should one decide what level of quality to purchase?

Sometimes people conclude that an expensive lifestyle is almost mandatory and there is nothing they can do about it. Young people sometimes unwillingly spend excessive amounts of money for clothing because they think they have to, to be accepted by their peers. Some have been told to quit objecting to it and just do it.

Unfortunately it's not just the young people who fall into this trap, and it's certainly not limited to apparel. But there is a wide scope of choice in clothing, from the latest styles and expensive trade names, to inexpensive but good, used items. A good plan is to buy for modesty, comfort and common sense. Dress to be warm, not to be "cool." Fads and carnal trends are a dead-end fleshly appeal, and cannot bring fulfillment for the soul, usually not even for the earthly senses.

13. Is it ever justifiable to pay two, three, or even four times as much for an "in" brand of clothes, watches, sunglasses, tools, or other things?
14. How does one find the common sense and personal fortitude to buy shoes to fit the feet rather than the head?
15. Does Isaiah 3:16-17 apply to the preceding question?

Another spending problem comes from the misplaced love that 2 Timothy 3:4 talks about. It says that some will be lovers of pleasure more than of God. The love and pursuit of pleasure is closely connected to money. It is usually expensive and also mind consuming. Proverbs 21:17 says, "He that loveth pleasure shall be a poor man."

16. Is all spending for pleasure out of place?
17. If not, what is a safe guide?

Exodus 32:1-6 speaks more specifically about pleasure seeking. When Moses was delayed on the mountain, the children of Israel made themselves a golden calf, and then among other things, "they sat down to eat and to drink, and rose up to play." It insinuates that there was something wrong about their eating as well as the playing.

According to numerous scriptures about this issue, we can conclude that this problem and related concerns are not a new issue. It does appear, though, that the problem is magnified in proportion to today's levels of affluence. According to statistics, U.S. citizens currently spend more for beverages than for utilities.

Eating can be a problem at home and in restaurants. Too much emphasis on food can create numerous problems. Eating out for the sake of eating out, especially group dining for social recreation, is a luxury. People eat away from home for many reasons, and there is a wide scope of how much people spend, from economic but nourishing meals to extravagant feasting.

So, pertaining especially to eating out, or dining away from home:

18. When is it acceptable?
19. For what reasons?
20. How often?
21. At what kinds of places?
22. For how much?
23. What criteria do you use to decide?
24. Check out Romans 16:18 in relation to this subject. (Don't skip this.)

Philippians 3:18-19 says, "For many walk, of whom I have told you often, and now tell you even weeping, that they are the enemies of the cross of Christ: Whose end is destruction, whose God is their belly, and whose glory is in their shame, who mind earthly things."

25. In our day and age, who are those, if anyone, whose god is their belly?
26. What is their guilt?

Returning to Exodus 32:6 after the people were done eating, they rose up to play. This is speaking about the adults. The inclination "to rise up and play" has not vanished nor diminished with the passing of time. Today many adults spend much time, money and effort for entertainment, retreats, recreations, and playing.

A great abundance of things cater to the world of play. These things range from small simple things, complex electronic items, to elaborate and expensive machines. It has been said, "The difference between the men and the boys is the size of their toys." Is that true?

27. An old adage says, "When the cat's away, the mice will play." Would this also apply to the issue of adults at play, meaning that when restraints are removed, they will play?
28. Can the ability to afford something seem to make it acceptable?
29. Should amusement parks be able to make profits from dedicated Christians?
30. Now reconsider question #4: Is game playing by adults a wise use of time? If so; why, when, under what circumstances.
31. Purchasing fireworks is a literal way to blow your money; why would it be on one's expense list?

Today there are toys, toys and more toys for children. Amazing amounts of money are spent for toys. In addition to durable items, Americans spend tens of billions of dollars yearly for disposable toys, those expected to last one year or less.

Many children receive far too many toys, and most times the parents and grandparents are at fault. Sometimes parents are more intrigued with a toy than their children are and will buy what their children don't even want, often with money that belongs elsewhere. An excess of toys tends to detract from children's contentment and hinder the development of ingenuity in a child. When children have few toys, they have to improvise and use their imagination to play with simple and basic things. This enhances ingenuity and resourcefulness.

32. What is responsible spending for toys?
33. What are some hindrances of too many toys?
34. What amount of toys is excessive?
35. Is this worse if parents buy even if they can't afford it?
36. What can parents do when they have convictions on the matter, but others keep bringing in the toys?
37. How can parents decide if a toy is a benefit or a hindrance?

In these times of affluence, the great majority of households have pets, and a large industry exists to provide for them. Many receive excessive attention and care, and cost owners lots of money that often should be used elsewhere.

Apparently people have had pets for a long time. "For every kind of beasts, and of birds, and of serpents, and of things in the sea, is tamed, and hath been tamed of mankind" (James 3:7). Some were tamed for work and likely many were tamed for pets and other reasons. Today people have a variety of pets though dogs are likely the most common. There is a saying that a dog is a man's best friend, yet in the Scriptures dogs seem to be referred to in a negative way.

38. Is there any significance to the quote in Revelation 22:15, "for without are dogs"?
39. Does the phrase "inordinate affection" in Colossians 3:5 have anything to do with this subject?
39. What extent of expense and care for pets is acceptable for Christians?

Americans (and some other nationalities) are said to have love affairs with cars. Do you? When cars became practical, Christians accepted them as a satisfactory means of transportation but felt that they should buy practical, modest and economic models. A costly car that is a status symbol becomes an issue of worldliness. Such a car is usually a rich person's car and is unsuitable for a conscientious Christian. Unnecessary vehicles can be a result of irresponsible spending and a drain on your finances. Most young single men and some older folk, for example, don't really need a car and a pick-up. As a person becomes more intent on being a Christian, the importance of model or style and the status symbol of a car should become less. Wise youth will look beyond their personal desires and urges to decide when, what kind, and by what means to buy a car.

40. For all age groups, what is your guide?

Good means of travel and affluent times make it easy to take to the road, but this brings new challenges. Don't travel too much or when you shouldn't. It can make you poor. It's not only the cost of traveling that's a problem, but also the cost of missed wages.

41. How does one decide when, where and why to take time off from work and how much to spend for traveling?
42. Is it ever acceptable to just go (to a funeral for instance) and figure out later how you will pay for the trip?
43. Do some people stay home too much?

Every now and then wedding bells start chiming, and you are invited to the wedding. Often there will be travel expenses, and culture demands that you take a gift. There are bridal showers, farewell parties, and other activities that also seem to require a gift and some of your time. All of this takes money.

It has been said that people will spend money they don't have, to buy things people don't need, to give to their friends who don't know what to do with them.

44. When you go out to buy a gift, how do you decide how much to spend?
45. What standards should one follow to choose a gift?

Cultural and peer pressure appears to almost demand an expensive honeymoon. Although much may be said in favor of a honeymoon, it far too often puts a financial stress on the young couple from day one. Sometimes it also brings other stresses to those first days of their marriage.

The idea that one will get married only once does not justify careless and lavish spending for honeymoons, sometimes to the point of borrowing for the occasion. This can indeed bring long-term negative consequences.

In the past, marriages were solid and successful, and just as happy, or even happier, without honeymoon travels and splurges. Today many young couples travel far and wide on extensive honeymoons. Is it doing any good for marriages and homes?

46. Are there Bible principles that apply to this subject?

It is said that everyone needs to have some type of a hobby, some sort of a collection, or some kind of diversion for the mind.

47. Is there any God-sanctioned truth to this idea?
48. If so, what is acceptable?

Ecclesiastes 7:2, addressing funerals, says, "It is better to go to the house of mourning, than to go to the house of feasting: *for that is the end of all men*; and the living will lay it to his heart."

49. How much is responsible and acceptable spending for a funeral?

Some funeral directors say that well-adjusted families with a healthy bond tend to spend less for a funeral of a family member than those who are loose-knit, or with stress and tensions. This is supposedly true even for Christians.

One funeral director's counsel is to "remember that whatever you do now is only for you. You cannot do anything more for the deceased."

50. What might be the reason that well-adjusted families spend less?
51. What should determine the expense for the funeral of a family member?

Finally, remember to ask God to give you His Holy Spirit to guide you in the many and sometimes perplexing decisions that need to be made in real life. Well-grounded, knowledgeable convictions and the grace of God are the secret of strength and wisdom, for all age groups, to overcome the pressures of the world and to be good stewards and responsible spenders.

Temperance
CHAPTER 17

The virtue of temperance (being modest and controlled) has much to do with the preceding subject of responsible spending, as well as with most of the other topics in this book. First Corinthians 9:25 speaks of the spiritual race as it relates to our life on the earth: "Every man that striveth for the mastery is temperate in all things."

1. What is included in the term, *all things*?
2. Must this virtue always be taught and learned?

First Peter 4:4 speaks about temperance in the reverse form, where it says that worldly minded people looking on "think it strange that ye run not with them to the same excess of riot, speaking evil of you." This verse serves as a good definition for the word temperance: self-restraint or abstinence from excess.

3. What guide can we go by to identify excess as it relates to the lack of temperance in finances and lifestyle?
4. What is the problem if your fellow churchgoers or family members seem to think it strange if you don't run or do with them?

Matthew 23:24 speaks about gnats and camels. It's about getting hung up on little things but ignoring much more important issues.

5. Does this have anything to do with temperance?
6. If so, what?

It is in order to be cautious, lest we get caught up in an absorbing desire to "fare sumptuously every day." This would be indicated by things like a selfish and luxurious lifestyle; a rich diet and much feasting; world-class clothing; excessive house furnishings and home decor; too much recreation and play; and other such things.

The certain rich man we read about in Luke 16:19 was not necessarily wrong because of what he had; the problem was that he was selfish and unconcerned about the poor man at his gate.

7. What can keep us from stumbling into that certain rich man's faults?
8. What is temperance when you go grocery shopping?
9. How is temperance best accomplished at the dining table?
10. Read Luke 21:34 and Proverbs 23:2, 20-21. How do these scriptures relate to temperance?

"Let your moderation be known unto all men. The Lord is at hand. Be careful for nothing; but in everything by prayer and supplication with thanksgiving let your requests be made known unto God" (Phil. 4:5-6).

11. Is moderation the same thing as temperance?
12. What does it mean to let your moderation *be known* to everyone?

Some say, "with money comes new light." With changing economics, some lifestyle changes might be acceptable; however, having plenty does not justify lavish, intemperate living. The virtue of temperance applies to the principle of buying according to one's needs, in modesty, simplicity, and with economic carefulness, whether one has little or much.

13. Does the issue of temperance change as a person gets more financial means?
14. What is the difference between new light and new reasoning?
15. Are some changes to our lifestyle acceptable as we have more funds available?
16. Is it okay to upgrade possessions just because we can handle it financially?

This is another subject that requires on-going perception because of the changing scenes of life. This is only a small touch on the issue, so keep your mind's eye open.

Business Ethics and Values

CHAPTER 18

When Christians go out to do business, they should have a goal of being reasonable and pleasant customers or clients. Businessmen should be glad to see you come back. This includes many facets of business associations. It includes your general conduct and keeping your children in control while you are in their place of business.

Don't be a hard, demanding bargain driver. It is biblical to keep the merchant's welfare in mind, as well as your own. The Bible does not indicate that Christians or any church group deserve special privileges or better deals than anyone else. It's better not to always push for the *absolute best* deal. Within God's policies, it's not necessary for success. This has been proven by faithful men. After all, a true bargain is a fair deal for both the buyer and the seller.

Far beyond thinking that we always deserve the best deals is the scriptural teaching that we should be willing to be cheated, if necessary. "Why do ye not rather take wrong? why do ye not rather suffer yourselves to be defrauded?" (1 Cor. 6:7). Also, Jesus taught that we should "Bless them that curse you, and pray for them which despitefully use you" (Luke 6:28). This is a world apart from demanding top-dollar deals and royal treatment from others.

1. Is there always something wrong with us if our appearance causes a merchant to think, Oh, my, there comes that person again!
2. What makes people think they deserve special privileges or better deals?
3. What is required to actually live by the scriptures quoted above?
4. Is it ever right to say, I'll never do business at that place again?

When it's in your power to set the price or specify the terms and conditions of a business deal, take care lest selfishness, greed or even dishonesty slip in. Be cautious also about extortion, which is exacting or forcing more than what is right or fair. Don't be inconsiderate, thinking only of your own gain or welfare.

Many scriptures apply to this issue. "Look not every man on his own things, but every man also on the things of others" (Phil. 2:4). "A false balance is abomination to the Lord: but a just weight is his delight" (Prov. 11:1). "Providing for honest things, not only in the sight of the Lord, but also in the sight of men" (2 Cor. 8:21).

5. Can you quote other scriptures that apply to this subject?
6. Would it help us to always consider the issue as if the tables were turned about?
7. The Golden Rule certainly applies to this subject. Why do people forget it so easily?
8. In business between brethren, close friends or relatives, who may expect more or less of whom?
9. Do you ever consider paying your brother or friend extra because of who they are?

Do not fall into the trap of misrepresenting what you want to buy or sell. Proverbs 24:14 says, "It is naught, it is naught, saith the buyer: but when he is gone his way, then he boasteth." This speaks about finding fault with an item when you want to buy it, later gloating about how cheap you got it, and finally boasting about its value when you want to sell it. "The getting of treasures by a lying tongue is a vanity tossed to and fro of them that seek death" (Prov. 21:6).

Misrepresentation can occur in many ways, sometimes even by lying with silence.

10. Is it always wrong to point out the faults of an item, just so you can buy it cheaper?
11. When you suspect that the seller is misrepresenting the item, what should you do?

Why do people in general, even Christians, tend to be careless about bills and borrowed items they owe each other? The person who lent an item should not have to ask for it to be returned. If someone has given you a loan, little or big, he should not have to ask for re-payment. Pay your dues promptly and cheerfully. After all, "the borrower is servant to the lender" (Prov. 22:7).

Whether the lender is in need of what you have borrowed has nothing to do with your obligation to return or repay it. Commitments and agreements are binding regardless of how you perceive the lender's circumstances. This is an especially sensitive issue between fellow church members and relatives.

12. Why do obligations to individuals seem less important or binding than obligations to businesses, banks and other institutions?
13. What should the lender do if the borrower does not keep his commitment?
14. Do you think Matthew 18:15-17 has the answer for the preceding question?

Exodus 22:14 gives some Old Testament rules about renting and borrowing, and specifically about responsibility for broken things or the death of an animal. It says, "And if a man borrow ought of his neighbour, and it be hurt, or die, the owner thereof being not with it, he shall surely make it good." Second Kings 6:5, describes the dismay of the builder as an ax head disappeared into the river: "alas ... *it was borrowed*." Apparently the man felt strongly duty-bound to return the borrowed ax, or perhaps provide a new one if he could not retrieve it.

15. Is this principle carried over into the New Testament?
16. Does a "what if" agreement beforehand help to avoid problems if things go wrong?

To make a business agreement and commitment of any kind, record it in writing, the more detailed the better, complete with signatures and dates, and file it in a place that is safe and easy to remember. Then set your mind to abide by it, and keep your promise, even when it hurts or costs you money. Psalm 15:1-2 and 4 speaks about a person who will take full responsibility for his commitments, even if it costs him dearly: "Lord, who shall abide in thy tabernacle? who shall dwell in thy holy hill? He that walketh uprightly, and worketh righteousness, and speaketh the truth in his heart. He that sweareth to his own hurt, and changeth not."

Let your *yes* mean yes (James 5:12). This is an important part of establishing a reputation that you can be trusted. It is an essential part of being "of good report" (1 Tim. 3:7).

Recording an agreement is especially important when it entails sizable amounts of money or involves a lengthy or unspecified duration of time. People do forget what they agreed to though sometimes they just become careless about the agreement. And sometimes, unfortunately, selfishness complicates the issue, and someone may actually want to forget.

17. What makes people reluctant to record an agreement or think that it's not necessary?
18. There are times when things have been properly recorded and problems arise anyway. Then what should you do?
19. Paper is not a cure-all, but it sure helps! Right?

In 1879 a man traveled 1300 miles by horseback to Bozeman, Montana, to repay a $300 loan. His friends urged him to just forget it. "They will never find you," they told him. He insisted, however, that he had to return and make good on his promise. Thereby he purchased to himself a good reputation.

To live a life that earns one a reputation *of good report* (1 Tim. 3:7) is of great value and has the potential of bringing many blessings to such a person. These blessings include a wide scope of things and circumstances.

20. Can you share an experience of your own or someone you know that illustrates this fact?

PARTNERSHIPS

Business partnerships are not a modern idea. Ecclesiastes 4:9 says, "Two are better than one; because they have a good reward for their labour." This verse implies that a partnership can be beneficial and rewarding. Financial profits, however, might be only part of the good reward mentioned. Hopefully there would be other benefits. Sometimes two or more working together make a situation more favorably workable. In some cases a joint venture can make the difference in whether or not a venture will succeed.

Luke 5:10 records a fishermen's partnership: "James, and John, the sons of Zebedee, which were partners with Simon." Apparently this was at least a three-way partnership. It may have been an alliance based on the need for manpower. Whatever the reason, they were partners.

There are many father-and-son partnerships. This can be an ideal way to phase in a new generation as the older one phases out.

Before organizing a partnership, it is important to seriously consider several issues.

- All reasons, ideas and goals should be well thought out from a spiritual and scriptural viewpoint.
- A Christian partnership must be scripturally ethical and legal according to the laws of the land. Review Romans 13 and 1 Peter 2:13, 14 and 17.
- Assign responsibility for the various parts of the operation. People's talents are not alike and some are more suited for one thing and some for another. 1 Corinthians 12:4-11 describes the spiritual aspect of this. To a large extent the same is true in the natural sense. One might be gifted at maintenance and repairs, another at bookkeeping, yet another at organizing, etc. Some ventures will have distinct lines between the operations of the business that make nice divisions of responsibilities. In others, the partners will need to work shoulder to shoulder.
- Give serious thought to social issues and the possible need to closely blend two or more families. Sometimes parents blend well, but when their children enter the scene, problems develop. Planning for this issue will be a big deterrent to problems.
- Business partnerships need detailed, written and signed agreements, of which everyone has a copy. This is addressed by the question in Amos 3:3: "Can two walk together, except they be agreed?"
- Planned, routine communication about circumstances and numbers is necessary for success.
- In all partnerships, as well as in all other business and related socializing, avoid the unequal yoke referred to in 2 Corinthians 6:14-15. This becomes an especially sensitive issue if one partner loses the Christian way.

- Because all partnerships will end, partnership agreements must include a dissolution plan to be complete. The end of a partnership is a more critical and sensitive time than the beginning. Much trouble can be averted if you plan how to settle affairs when that day comes. Sometimes, depending on circumstances, it is wise to set the duration of the partnership and the date of, or reason for termination.
- When the day comes for the dissolution or rearranging of a partnership, the Golden Rule in Matthew 7:12 becomes extremely important. This applies whether you are selling your share, purchasing a partner's share, or making other changes or settlement. If you are requesting a certain settlement, consider seriously how your offer would appeal to you if your partner were offering you that deal. Remember the law of sowing and reaping (Gal. 6:7).
- Seeking counsel and advice from outside sources can help prevent problems and insure success.
- Last but far from least, be prepared to take full responsibility for your commitments and to keep your promises and agreements completely, even if you need to take wrong or suffer loss because of it. See Psalm 15:1-4, and 1 Corinthians 6:1-7.

BEING IN BUSINESS

Following is a list of things to consider when you are the businessperson behind the counter. It is, of course, not all-inclusive, and there are issues that are specific to various types of businesses. However, common sense application of Bible principles goes a long way to help make any honorable business succeed.

- Aim to run your business in humility and with simplicity.
- Be a pleasure to do business with. Give people a good reason to want to come back.
- Do your best to deal kindly and respectfully with problems and unhappy customers.
- Endeavor to exceed your customer's expectation; promise less and do more.
- Always be truthful and tell it like it is. Don't make phony excuses.
- Be consistent in your approach and ideals. Avoid abrupt or radical changes.

- Give honest and ample weight and measure.
- Keep your place of business clean and organized. It will yield productive effects.
- Never think you need or deserve all the business. Allow room for others in life.
- Never resort to extortion and greed, which can close one's door into the kingdom of God. See 1 Corinthians 6:9-10.
- Pay your bills on or before time. Usually you will enjoy advantages because of it.
- Forgive offenders. Remember those times when you needed forgiveness.
- Don't let your business consume you mentally, physically, socially or spiritually. Keep your real goals and ideals prominently in view.

Several scriptures relate directly to being in business and teach that God demands fairness. "Thou shalt not have in thy bag divers weights, a great and a small. Thou shalt not have in thine house divers measures, a great and a small. But thou shalt have a perfect and just weight, a perfect and just measure shalt thou have: that thy days may be lengthened in the land which the Lord thy God giveth thee. For all that do such things, and all that do unrighteously, are an abomination unto the Lord thy God" (Deut. 25:13-15). "A false balance is abomination to the Lord: but a just weight is his delight" (Prov. 11:1).

1. Should Christians be able to rise above the temptation to ever shade the facts or pad the weight?

Pay your bills on time. It is poor policy to habitually wait beyond the last day and use up all grace periods, actual or assumed. Be especially careful to promptly pay your fellow church member, your brother, or any other relatives or friends. The same goes for any church organizations or charitable organizations to which you owe any payments. These are of utmost importance. Early or prompt payment of your dues will in the long run bring advantages and blessings. Conversely, always being delinquent and untrustworthy with your obligations eventually places you outside the canopy of God's blessing.

2. Is the practice of letting bills run past due, consciously or even intentionally, like stealing other people's money for the duration of the past-due period?
3. What is the duty of fellow church members who are aware of such a problem?
4. Why is there such a problem with late, ignored, or forgotten payments to family members, friends, and fellow church members?
5. When does late payment become a sin?

The discipline of punctuality in business doings bears positive fruit also in non-business obligations such as deadlines, mealtimes, church attendance, social appointments, church-related paper work, and a host of other things.

6. Is paying a bill late worse than being late for an appointment?
7. Is habitual tardiness a spiritual problem or a temperament dilemma?

Do not resort to bribery for selfish gain. It's not God's way. "For I know your manifold transgressions and your mighty sins: they afflict the just, they take a bribe (plus other things)" (Amos 5:12). "Keep me from bloody men...whose hands are full of mischief and bribes" (Ps. 26:8-11). The problem of bribery has not disappeared with the passing of time. The suggestion or temptation may surface at unexpected times and instances.

8. Is any type of bribery or pay-off acceptable?
9. What is the key keeping power for Christians to stay clean from bribery?

Proper customer service is important from the biblical standpoint as well as for success. You stand a small chance of success if you cannot or do not keep at least most of your customers satisfied most of the time. Take note of the term *customer service.* If your thoughts and goals are primarily for yourself, you will likely portray "self" service instead of customer service. If you focus mostly on profits instead of on supporting yourself by offering an honorable service, you greatly diminish your chances of success.

It costs much more to attract new customers than to keep existing ones. Customer recommendation, or word of mouth, is the cheapest and the best advertisement. It is important to keep your customers happy, especially first-time customers, so they will come back and will spread a good word for you.

An unhappy and dissatisfied customer will, it is said, tell an average of nine people about their gripes. That is significantly more than a satisfied customer will tell about their good impression. However, if you do what it takes to resolve the problem or conflict, on the spot if possible, most complaining customers will do business with you again.

Therefore, "agree with thine adversary quickly," before they go elsewhere with their business and influence others to also stay away. In addition, and more importantly, according to the Scriptures, it is the right thing to do.

10. Quote some scriptures that apply to this subject. (There are many.)
11. What can one do for the few complaining customers who seem determined to leave with a grudge?
12. Are there some that actually cannot be satisfied no matter how hard you try?

As a rule, if you deal fairly with people, they will be fair with you. "Who is he that will harm you, if ye be followers of that which is good?" (1 Pet. 3:13). If you prove yourself to be honest, they will normally trust you. This gives justice a chance to prevail and should be a great advantage for all in the end. These qualities will give you the best likelihood of finding joy in your service to others.

13. If one just can't seem to find joy in their service or business, should he quit?

Much care must be taken and perhaps a lot counsel sought in choosing a business venture or an occupation because the lure of profits can easily distort a person's spiritual vision and sense of integrity. This can also occur in the normal daily business doings. The opportunity of gain has often enticed people to override their conscience and justify things that they knew were not in order or not right for them.

14. What is needed for a Christian to become immune to the enticement of unsanctioned profits?

Certain types or sizes of business ventures are sometimes referred to as *risky business*, insinuating a high chance of major problems or failure.

15. From a Christian point of view, what are those?
16. Is it ever in order for Christian people to take recognized, serious risks in an effort to get a fast jump ahead?

Pyramid sales programs need close scrutiny. These are programs in which each person recruits others to sell, and then receives a percentage of their sales. Those he recruits then enlist more sellers from whose sales he also gets a percentage. This is often carried to the third and sometimes a fourth level. There is a variety of this type of plans. Most of them thrive by appealing to people with a desire to get rich rapidly. They usually make lofty promises and tout big gains with virtually no investment and little effort; because those you recruit are supposed to do the selling and you reap the profits.

Normally these programs require an intensive commitment for a person to succeed. The promise of huge and quick profits is usually more prominent than the value of the product. This system of marketing has been, and still is, controversial among Christians. Though it may not be fair to pass a blanket judgment against these programs, most of them seem to have a questionable foundation and dubious business practices. Therefore serious thought needs to be given to this issue before becoming involved. Seeking counsel from others would be very wise.

17. If you agree with these thoughts, how should you think concerning those who are deeply involved?
18. If you disagree, what is your reasoning and explanation?

Don't fall for get-rich-quick gimmicks and other unfair or unethical programs. They come in many forms and might get your attention in many different ways. Many promise near-instant wealth if you will only send them a given amount of money. Those who fall for these programs end up poorer, not richer. There are also chain letter scams that promise quick, easy money. The only way anyone can profit by these is by the losses of others. Many people have stumbled and been trapped by these scams, resulting in big losses and serious disappointments.

Following are some ideas to consider in relation to easy money.

- "Wealth *gotten* by vanity shall be diminished: but *he that gathereth by labour* shall increase" (Prov.13-11).
- Remember, if it sounds too good to be true, it probably is.
- "The simple believeth every word: but the prudent man looketh well to his going" (Prov. 14:15).
- "I send you forth as sheep in the midst of wolves: *be ye therefore wise as serpents*, and harmless as doves" (Matt. 10:16).

19. Are there more gimmicks or other issues that may need warnings or teaching about how to help people stay out of trouble?
20. What does it take to earn the title of being a *prudent man* (Prov. 14:15)?

Christians should not need to participate in questionable programs or unethical practices to make their living. God has much better ways to sustain and bless His children. "He that tilleth his land shall have plenty of bread: but he that followeth after vain persons shall have poverty enough. A faithful man shall abound with blessings: but he that maketh haste to be rich shall not be innocent" (Prov. 12:11 and 28:19, 20). In today's language it means he that faithfully works his job or applies himself to his occupation will be blessed by God with provisions for life.

IN ALL THY WAYS ACKNOWLEDGE HIM,
AND HE SHALL DIRECT THY PATHS.
PROVERBS 3:6

Lending and Borrowing

CHAPTER 19

For a long, long, time people have been borrowing from those willing to lend to them. There are various reasons why people lend their possessions, and many reasons why others desire to borrow. There is much teaching in the Bible about the different subtitle subjects and for everyone involved.

DEBT

Debt is an old subject, and the Bible has lots to say about it. It does not say that having debt is a sin. It's why or for what, how much and what you do about it that makes the difference of right or wrong. What your debt does to you is also a matter of concern.

Today there seems to be little or no fear of debt, and most people of North America have accepted a heavy debt load as normal and unavoidable. But debts do not just happen, and bills do not just occur out of the blue. They are normally the result of choices you make. Good credit is nice to have but costly to use. It is easy to draw on, but can be very difficult to repay.

In one sense general debt is much like a credit card. Both are debt taken on by choice and can serve as a tool to accomplish a goal. However, just like many tools, voluntary debt can be dangerous. It can bring on circumstances you didn't plan for and that you may not like.

Excessive debt with its stress and interest expense should not be the Christian's way of life. Except for unavoidable misfortune or circumstances brought on by God, spiritual priorities and proper self-discipline should keep Christians from accepting or ending up with huge and chronic debt loads.

1. If large debts do not cause stress for a person, does that mean he is careless about it?
2. Why or in what way can voluntary debt be so dangerous?
3. Much teaching and warning has been done about undue debt. Why is it still a problem?

Interest expense on debt can rapidly eat up your income. Monthly payments, or your creditor, can quickly become your master. Debt can easily become a hard taskmaster and it can occur before people realize what's happening. That's some of the problem with debt.

Many people in North America are driven by debt payments. This force may be somewhat mysterious and can do a variety of things to people. The payments are due every month, like an incessantly dripping faucet (drip - drip - drip - drip . . .) regardless of your circumstances. A Russian proverb says, "Debt and misery live on the same road."

Remember, "The rich ruleth over the poor, and *the borrower is servant to the lender*" (Prov. 22:7). Accepting payments on debt is, to a degree, yielding to servitude.

A medical study about stress and depression concluded that "the more vibrant and healthy inner spirituality a person has, the less likely he is to be seriously in debt."

4. What is a healthy fear of debt?
5. How should Christians feel about the *driving force* brought on by debts?
6. What is being "seriously in debt"?
7. How should personal spirituality influence or regulate one's debt loads?

There is a difference between equitable and manageable debt and excessive debt. Following are some points to help define excessive debt:

- First and foremost, more debts than value of assets
- More payments than cash flow
- More debt than can reasonably be paid off in your normal earning years
- No margin for any problems
- So much debt that it becomes a driving, enslaving force

- More than God can bless
- So much debt that it causes you to override your spiritual direction

DEBTORS

Debt is serious business! Excessive debt is one problem, and delinquent debt is yet another one. According to Psalm 37:21, it is wickedness to borrow (or rent) and then not pay. This fact forbids slothfulness in repaying and rules out elective bankruptcy for Christians.

However, in life it happens that sometimes Christian people end up with huge debts, far beyond the value of their assets. Sometimes the situation is so serious that there seems little or no hope of ever getting out of debt. Sometimes it is the result of an act of God or some type of misfortune, and sometimes it's due to serious mismanagement or other faults.

1. How should the person caught in such a situation feel about it?
2. May they expect others to come running to help them out, especially if it's a case of a personal fault?
3. If it requires long years of labor to pay the debts, is it okay to sometimes get discouraged about everything?
4. How shall the onlookers think about it?
5. Do you think God would want more people to be less self-centered and more willing to help those in trouble, perhaps with an interest-free loan or a gift?

If you actually cannot make your payment, at least talk to your creditor. It is your duty to go (or to call) before you are delinquent, admit your problem, and explain your circumstances. Irresponsible financial delinquency is a serious fault. Christians should do everything within their power to avoid this.

A senior bank loan officer said, "If people in trouble are willing to communicate, in almost every case, some workable plan of action can be negotiated. But if they do not talk about their problems, and if they don't answer the telephone, or their mail, then we have a serious problem."

In a community where Mennonites were new, a Mennonite man ran into serious financial difficulties due to misfortune beyond his control. When he realized he was in trouble, he alerted his banker and arranged a meeting with him and a number of brethren from his church. They came up with a plan of action that in the end proved successful. As the banker was leaving, he expressed his appreciation for the meeting and the way this man's spiritual brothers stood by him, helping to find a workable plan. He said he had never before witnessed anything like it.

6. What is it that makes people stay silent or hide the facts when things are not working out?
7. Is the above illustration what Proverbs 24:6-b speaks about?
8. What other Bible principles are in action in this illustration?

Many people resort to living against the limit financially, and otherwise. This often includes borrowing to the limit and accepting long-term commitments to rigorous payment plans. Heavy debt loads, even though legitimate, often leave no margin for error or problems and can be the cause of many stresses and limits in your life.

Debt can keep you from being a Good Samaritan. It can limit or even prohibit many other forms of religious activities or humanitarian service. It keeps many from giving time in mission service, voluntary service units, etc., or even just helping a neighbor.

Frequently, extensive debt hinders men from being good husbands and fathers. To be sure, it affects women also. And unfortunately it can be a drawback that can, without doubt, keep a man from flourishing as a minister or a deacon.

9. What comments have you to add to these thoughts?
10. Does 2 Timothy 2:4 shed any light on the subject?

Young men (and ladies), don't be overly concerned about quickly establishing credit so you can borrow money or sign up for charge cards, etc. When you do have borrowing credit established, use it reluctantly and cautiously and guard it with your integrity. Your credit report will tell others a lot about your true character.

Young men should think very seriously about getting married with a heavy debt load, especially so if they have insufficient assets to show for it, and then expect their wives to assume a share of the responsibility. Young ladies, you are allowed to inquire about this issue. It can have a big impact on your marriage and life in general.

11. How responsible are parents for their son's financial situation when he wants to get married?
12. Should the parents of the girl make it their business to help their daughter find out about these facts?

Whether you are young or already older, you can avoid many debt problems if you borrow cautiously—only when necessary. Don't let the opportunity to borrow make you bold and reckless in your earthly pursuits. Do not yield to the temptation to live rich on borrowed money. Many people have gotten into financial trouble because they gave in to their desires to have everything they wanted *right now*! If you do any of these things, you will likely suffer for it, perhaps severely and for a long time.

13. Can one be overly cautious or unduly fearful about assuming debt?

To stay out of debt and succeed with your finances, you must avoid always kicking the heels of your earning power. If you do not maintain a distance or margin between your earnings and your spending, you will always be broke.

Making the money reach around is usually more easily accomplished by spending less than earning more. Normally you have (or should have), more control over your spending than your earning. By reducing your spending, avoiding waste and cutting out your wants, you can in effect raise your income. To accomplish this, however, requires the maturity and willingness to plan frugally.

14. Are the last two paragraphs true?
15. Can you share any illustrations or experiences that relate to the issue?

If you are overloaded with debt, don't give in to temptations to occasionally go on a "get-away trip"; it will only make matters worse. Much better, go on a "get help" mission. To be helped successfully though, you must actually want help.

15. Why do get-away trips worsen the problem?
16. Is there a way to help someone who doesn't think they need help?

Debt counselors (and some deacons) say that debt consolidation loans generally do not work and are usually not a successful lasting answer for debt overloads.

17. Why not?
18. What is the answer then?

CREDIT CARD USE

Credit cards can be a handy tool, but they are also quite dangerous. Responsible use of credit cards takes a lot of self-control and careful management. Without personal fortitude, many people end up with many cards and with huge balances due. This has caused many financial disasters.

To avoid a card disaster, fix it firmly in your mind that your credit limit on your card is not available money; it is only available debt. That's it! Credit cards are convenient, but they can be hazardous. Total monthly pay off is a must for practical use.

If you have any favorable credit history at all (sometimes even if you do not) you will have to resist tempting credit card offers. Keep in mind that the banks issuing the credit cards are not interested in your welfare; their goal is to get a share your money. Just remember, when you sign on their line, you are responsible for what happens next.

1. What other key issues would help people stay out of credit card problems?
2. What do parents owe their children in the use of credit cards?
3. Because of the era we live in, should parents help their children acquire a credit card before they leave home so they can teach them responsible use of it?

GETTING OUT OF DEBT

A desire to live debt-free is a legitimate goal and is often possible, sooner than people tend to think, provided they are serious about it and willing for the necessary procedures. Following is a list of some things to do to get out of debt.

A. Quit borrowing, and stop charging!

B. Seek advice and follow it.
C. Design a realistic payback plan and follow it.
D. If you haven't been giving to charitable causes, start now.
E. Buy only necessities, sparingly and cautiously, and pay as you go.
F. Practice self-restraint; be willing to make sacrifices; learn to do without some things.
G. Do something extra. Look for any sensible opportunities that will help pay your debts.
H. Trust in God and seek true spirituality.

CREDITORS

If you have the means, be willing to lend to those in need. Many people of means have been reluctant to give a lift for fear of not receiving payback or because of an unwillingness to approach the borrower if he does not keep the agreement.

When you lend to someone, you are, according to Proverbs 22:7, taking on the responsibility of having a servant. It says, "The borrower is servant to the lender."

When you are the creditor, and the borrower is not paying according to your agreement, you owe it to him to call him to account. "Moreover if thy brother shall trespass against thee, go and tell him his fault between thee and him alone" (Matt. 18:15). It is very important though, that you go with more concern for the other person's spiritual and financial well-being than anxiety about your own money.

1. How can the creditor maintain the proper attitude and right priorities?
2. What should the creditor do if he sees the borrower living high and spending lavishly instead of paying back promptly according to the agreement?

When all else fails, and your client is, for whatever reason, actually unable to repay you or simply does not pay, you must, according to the teachings of Jesus, forgive the debtor. See Matthew 18:23-35.

3. How can one attain the grace to freely forgive in such a case?

CO-SIGNING NOTES

The equivalent of co-signing bank loans appears to be an old practice. There are a number of direct scriptures from Proverbs about this subject. They seem to all discourage the practice or at least urge great caution.

"My son, if you become surety for your friend, If you have shaken hands in pledge for a stranger, You are snared by the words of your mouth; You are taken by the words of your mouth (or by the signing with your pen)" (Prov. 6:1-2).

"He that is surety for a stranger shall smart for it: and he that hateth suretyship is sure" (Prov. 11:15).

"A man void of understanding striketh hands, and becometh surety in the presence of his friend" (Prov. 17:18).

"Be not thou one of them that strike hands, or of them that are sureties for debts. If thou hast nothing to pay, why should he take away thy bed from under thee?" (Prov. 22:26-27).

The word *surety*, as used in these scriptures, means to take on responsibility for another person's commitment. In relation to bank loans, it is guaranteeing with your signature that you will pay the debt with your money if the borrower does not.

Knowing how to help someone with a legitimate need, without getting into trouble thereby might be another case of being as wise as a serpent but as harmless as a dove.

Many times borrowers do not realize the gravity of what they are asking a co-signer to do. And far too many people who co-sign a loan do not take seriously enough what they are doing. If you co-sign, you are agreeing that if they don't pay, you will, with your money, and there is no legal stipulation included that the borrower must then reimburse you.

It's a lot to ask from someone, and if you agree to do it, it's a serious and binding commitment.

1. Considering everything, should a person never do it?
2. Can you name other or better and safer ways to help out?

Government Issues and Taxes

CHAPTER 20

The Bible is not silent about our attitudes and responses to government issues. Beware of being an anti-government activist or a faultfinding complainer. First Peter 2:13-14, 17 says, "Submit yourselves to every ordinance of man for the Lord's sake: whether it be to the king, as supreme; Or unto governors, as unto them that are sent by him for the punishment of evildoers, and for the praise of them that do well. Honour all men. Love the brotherhood. Fear God. Honour the king."

1. What should Christians do when they see or hear that the government is not punishing evildoers?
2. How are we supposed to honor a president or any leader who is less than noble?

Titus 3:1-2 says, "Put them in mind to be subject to principalities and powers, to obey magistrates, to be ready to every good work, To speak evil of no man, to be no brawlers, but gentle, showing all meekness unto all men."

3. What quality can keep us from bad-mouthing the government, especially officials who appear to be tainted with corruption?
4. Psalm 35:20 uses this phrase: "them that are quiet in the land." In what way does this apply to government issues and Christians?

According to Romans 13:1-5, God is very much involved in national governments. "[1]Let every soul be subject unto the higher powers.

For there is no power but of God: the powers that be are ordained of God. [2]Whosoever therefore resisteth the power, resisteth the ordinance of God: and they that resist shall receive to themselves damnation. [3]For rulers are not a terror to good works, but to the evil. Wilt thou then not be afraid of the power? do that which is good, and thou shalt have praise of the same: [4]For he is the minister of God to thee for good. But if thou do that which is evil, be afraid; for he beareth not the sword in vain: for he is the minister of God, a revenger to *execute* wrath upon him that doeth evil. [5]Wherefore *ye* must needs be subject, not only for wrath, but also for conscience sake."

5. Does verse one about being subject mean that we must always be totally law-abiding?
6. Is the first sentence in verse three always true?
7. How would you explain verse four?
8. Verse five says we shall be subject, *not only for wrath*, or reluctantly and barely enough to stay out of trouble. What qualities or mind-set allows us to respect our government as an asset rather than a nuisance or even as an enemy?

Be especially careful about chafing at government requirements that you don't like, perhaps mostly because they cost you money. If your attitude about money is incorrect, government regulations can be a big problem. It might be a test of your integrity.

Also, use great caution not to become greedy or dishonest for gain through government assistance or support programs. Although a government that exercises a care for the people of the country is commendable, an abundance of assistance programs increases the tests of character for Christians.

Unfortunately even many Christians seem to be reluctant to pay their taxes, but are perhaps very quick, and overeager, to collect from government programs.

9. What scriptural criterion is a guide to decide which programs are acceptable for a Christian to participate in?
10. Rather than being too ready to accept, or even yearning for funds from the government, would it be better to have a little pride in one's self-supporting abilities?

The tax issue is a very important part of the government requirements to be considered, and the Bible is not silent about it. Taxation is an old, long-standing practice. Throughout the Old Testament we read about various types of taxation and government demands on the people. There have been times in history when demands and taxes were very harsh and unjust. However, as a rule, the Lord has always made a way for His people. Is that correct?

Jesus paid His taxes. In Matthew 17:24-27, there is a dialog specifically about the tax issue: "They that received tribute money came to Peter, and said, Doth not your master pay tribute? He saith, yes." After questioning Simon, Jesus told him, "Lest we should offend them, go thou to the sea, and cast an hook, and take up the fish that first cometh up; and when thou hast opened his mouth, thou shalt find a piece of money: that take, and give unto them for me and thee."

11. What have you to say about this incident?
12. Does this mean that the Lord will generally supply us with the funds to pay our taxes?

"For this cause pay ye tribute also: for they are God's ministers, attending continually upon this very thing. Render therefore to all their dues: tribute to whom tribute *is due*; custom to whom custom; fear to whom fear; honour to whom honour" (Rom. 13:6-7).

According to the Scriptures, an anti-tax mentality is not blessed by God. The Scriptures rather imply that we should pay our taxes *willingly*. This would include income taxes, property taxes, sales taxes, and perhaps quite a few others. When it says in Romans 13:8 that we should "owe no man anything," it surely also applies to the tax issue.

13. What is it that universally makes people reluctant or negative about paying taxes?
14. Are there any specific things one can do to overcome the root cause of complaining about taxes?
15. What should one say to others who express their aversion to paying their taxes?

In the *Martyrs Mirror*, page 1134, a letter from the Dutch authorities to the rulers of the Swiss city of Berne says that the Mennonites "have always with cheerful and willing mind rendered custom and taxes" and goes on to give them a reputation as a law-abiding and benevolent people.

16. Who qualifies for such a reputation today, and in what way is it most evident?

A foreigner stood in line with others to pay the real-estate taxes on his house. While others grumped and complained, this man appeared to be cheerful and free. When someone inquired about his attitude, he said, "In the country where I came from there was no chance for me to own a house like I have here, let alone have money to pay taxes on it. Now I have both. For this I am thankful and happy." What lesson is in this illustration for you?

Cultivating thankfulness for the benefits from your tax dollar should also help you cheerfully pay what is due and go on in life with a healthy attitude. A willingness to pay your taxes without complaining will have an encouraging effect on other areas of your life.

17. What might some of those encouraging effects be?

There are many types of sales taxes, and they vary from place to place. The fact that some of these taxes can be reduced or evaded by misstating facts has lured many people into dishonesty and wrongdoing.

18. What should keep a person completely honest in this issue when perhaps nobody would ever find out about it?
19. What should a Christian do when he feels pressured into a tax-dodging deal by another person?

Income taxes for self-employed people in the USA and Canada are largely based on self-calculated net income. This affords a temptation to manipulate figures in one's own favor in an effort to avoid taxation. Employees also encounter things and ways in which they can manipulate their net taxable income. Although there may be many times when there are no clear or absolute rules, these facts do bring about another test of character.

20. In those cases where there are no clear-cut rules, what should a Christian go by to know what is right in the sight of God?

To be free before God, it is necessary to give an honest report on all the forms when you file your income taxes. Taking advantage of balanced, legal and ethical tax planning is acceptable, but devious, unethical tax shelters and tax evasion are not.

21. Is the difference always evident?
22. Do you spend more time planning for your soul, than you do planning about taxes?
23. Is it acceptable for Christians to do everything they can to avoid paying income tax?
24. Does God expect us to be super careful not to pay any more taxes than we absolutely have to in order to be good stewards?
25. Is it okay for Christians to purposely wait until the last hour of the last day to file their income taxes or make necessary deposits, etc.?

Keep in mind that if you have a large amount of taxes to pay, you must have had large profits. It's much better to concern oneself with responsible use of the profits after the taxes, than to get hung up on the tax issue.

Dealing with Success and Failure

CHAPTER 21

Due to the makeup of humans, success and failure are both challenging and either one can be difficult to cope with. However, we are not left without direction for whichever the Lord allows or sends our way.

CONCERNING SUCCESS

One of the first things about success is to "remember that it is God that gives you the power to get wealth" (Deut. 8:18). That applies to people the world over, whether they honor God or not. The whole eighth chapter of Deuteronomy is pertinent to this subject. It appears that people are better able to cope with adversity than with success and prosperity, yet poverty has its own troubles and does not automatically make one righteous.

Another important mind-set is the warning in Psalm 62:10: "If riches increase, *set not your heart upon them*." This is about loving the things of the world too much, or even just feeling inordinate appreciation for one's possessions or status.

1. What does it mean to set one's heart upon his riches?

Not all success may be sanctioned by God. Ezekiel 28:5-10 starts out: "By thy great wisdom and by thy traffic hast thou increased thy riches, and thine heart is lifted up because of thy riches: Therefore thus saith the Lord God. . . ." It continues with a verdict of reaping for unsanctioned material increase.

2. What then is the ideal spiritual approach for balanced principles for everyday living?

Prosperity and abundance are not always signs of success, and poverty is not necessarily a sign of failure. There are people who have an abundance of possessions, but their lives do not work well, and many of them do not seem to have peace with God. Others just cannot seem to get ahead, sometimes for obvious reasons. Some have very little of this world's goods, but are supporting themselves and living successfully. And there are those whom God has prospered financially, who are also living faithfully and are at peace with God.

First Timothy 6:5 warns about drawing a wrong conclusion: "supposing that gain is godliness." On the other hand, concluding that poverty then must be godliness is just as incorrect.

3. How would you define success in general?
4. What do you consider *God-sanctioned* financial success?
5. On what do you base your thinking?
6. Does success have anything to do with contentment?

Most financial success stories do not just happen. They usually include lots of hard work, perseverance, self-discipline, time, and a structured lifestyle, including sufficient sleep. If you are not succeeding, don't excuse yourself because you're not a genius. Most successful people are said to have been B and C students in school, and many of the A's and B's end up working for the C's and D's.

7. Why is this?
8. How much should a person be concerned about being labeled as a success?
9. Frequently we hear the term "getting ahead." Ahead of what?

Before you have more than enough, learn to live by Holy Spirit convictions and common sense, not by your money or credit limits. This type of self-control prepares you to deal with success and possible surplus funds, if that is what God allows for you.

If you are successful in life, you will need to resist the temptation of an ego trip and beware that you don't take undue credit or honor to yourself or glory in your success. James 1:10 says that rich people shall stay humble, remembering that like flowers and grass, just like everyone else; they also will pass away. Second Corinthians 10:17-18 instructs, "But he that glorieth, let him glory in the Lord. For not he that commendeth himself is approved, but whom the Lord commendeth."

Consider Nebuchadnezzar's experience, when he thought that he by himself had accomplished his status "*by the might of my power, and for the honour of my majesty*" (Dan. 4:28-37). He didn't get by with it. He had a difficult lesson to learn.

Ezekiel 28:4-5 records the message to the prince of Tyrus: "With thy wisdom and with thine understanding thou hast gotten thee riches . . . and *thine heart is lifted up because of thy riches*." The verses following this spell out a grim reaping for wrongdoing.

Yet another warning is recorded in Deuteronomy 8:7-17, "For the Lord thy God bringeth thee into a good land... When thou hast eaten and art full . . . Beware that thou forget not the Lord thy God . . . And thou say in thine heart, *my power and the might of mine hand* hath gotten me this wealth." Many great men have come to ruin because of a wrong perception of themselves and their good circumstances.

10. Is this tendency in man the same today as it was back then?
11. Does God tend to wink at such attitudes in this age, or is He just tolerant and forgiving?
12. How can a successful person stay humble and keep a realistic and honest perception of himself and his accomplishments?
13. If and when things do start going well for a young man, what is the secret for him to stay clean in attitude? See Psalm 119:9.

In Mark 10:24, Jesus was again talking about "*them that trust in riches*."

14. How do people trust in riches? Give an example?

First Timothy 6:17-19 contains important, down-to-earth direction to those whose endeavors have been successful. "Charge them that are rich in this world, that they be not high minded, nor trust in uncertain riches, but in the living God, who giveth us richly all things to enjoy; That they do good, that they be rich in good works, ready to distribute, willing to communicate; Laying up in store for themselves a good foundation against the time to come, that they may lay hold on eternal life." And another real important scripture to remember is in Proverbs 22:2 where it says: The rich and poor meet together: the Lord is the maker of them all.

If and when you are successful to the point of having surplus means, don't neglect the gift of giving and helping. Be careful not to despise the poor. "And ye have respect to him that weareth the gay clothing, and say unto him, Sit thou here in a good place; and say to the poor, Stand thou there, or sit here under my footstool: Are ye not then partial in yourselves, and are become judges of evil thoughts? Hearken, my beloved brethren, Hath not God chosen the poor of this world rich in faith, and heirs of the kingdom which he hath promised to them that love him? But ye have despised the poor" (James 2:3-6).

15. What is required to be qualified to teach or coach others about this subject?
16. How shall we decide if and when to help some poor or unfortunate ones?
17. Are we always more in danger of being unwilling to help, or is it just as big a problem to be too quick to lend a hand or a dollar?

Be conscious of your mind-set when making plans for the future. James 4:13-15 says, "Go to now, ye that say, Today or tomorrow we will go into such a city, and continue there a year, and buy and sell, and get gain: Whereas ye know not what shall be on the morrow. For what is your life? It is even a vapour, that appeareth for a little time, and then vanisheth away. For that ye ought to say, If the Lord will, we shall live, and do this, or that."

Also we tend to ignore the fact that "Except the Lord build the house, they labor in vain who build it" (Ps. 127:1-2). (Or, except the Lord bless your efforts, you will work in vain.)

18. What reminders can help us remember these important facts?

One more item to consider about success is what Luke 19:8 says about Zaccheaus. It relates to succeeding, or at least profiting, at the expense of others or by any unfair practices. Unfortunately this can be done in many ways.

19. What is required of one who has miss-stepped in this way?
20. Was Zaccheaus rational in the commitment he declared?

CONCERNING FAILURE

Things are not always as they look to us. It appears that it is not God's plan for all people to be prosperous. Having the right attitude about this becomes a challenge for those who are having unsuccessful experiences. It is also a test for those successful ones looking on from their own place in life to keep a right attitude and to know what they should do or say or not say.

1. Why does God sometimes allow or even cause honest and well-intentioned plans and efforts to fail?
2. Is every case that appears like failure, actually that?

If your budget just doesn't seem to work or your business venture seems to be failing, the best thing to do is acknowledge it and go for help. Be careful about making quick or drastic and impulsive changes without proper council and support.

Perhaps life as a whole is just not going right. Do not go on a "get away from it all trip;" that normally only makes matters worse. In Isaiah 30:16, the prophet had a message for the people when things were not going well. They were encouraged to turn to God to be saved and find rest and quietness, but they said, "No; for we will flee upon horses." Apparently they thought they could outrun their troubles. But the answer is still the same today: "turn to God."

If you have "toiled all night" (or the whole year, or even many years) without success, it could be you need some instruction from the Lord to "cast your net *on the other side* of the boat." See John 21:1-11. In other words, sometimes people do need to make major changes and seek a totally different course to correct problems.

Sometimes man's good planning and best efforts fail because the Lord does not allow success. This can happen for a wide variety of reasons. Consider the tower of Babel, from Genesis 11:1-9. God was well able to keep the plan from succeeding.

3. When things are in fact not working, what is the danger about making quick or drastic changes?

4. Does it ever work to run away from troubles?

Sometimes an undue fear of failure has a paralyzing effect, and that fear can be the thing that will keep one from succeeding when he otherwise could. A hunter who cannot bring himself to take a shot for fear of missing will surely come home empty-handed. It can be much like this for people concerning necessary decisions and financial matters.

5. What can be done for a person who is stalled by fear of failure?

When things end up in disappointment, people sometimes become bitter about their circumstances. However, one possible silver lining of failure is the fact that most people learn much more from defeat, than they do from easy success or sweeping victory.

6. What mind-set makes it most possible for us to learn from our mistakes and defeats?
7. Do successful people have fewer learning opportunities?

Because of faulty makeup, people sometimes just plain fail, are at fault, and make a mess of their finances and other things. This sometimes happens even to people who sincerely want to be Christians and serve the Lord.

8. When this is the case, how are they responsible to God?
9. How responsible are they in making confessions, apologies, and restitution or repayments?
10. Does 2 Corinthians 7:11 apply to this issue?

One man failed miserably in numerous ways and was forced into bankruptcy, resulting in a large sum of unpaid debts. With conviction and diligence, however, he was able to pay all the old debts over time, even though such payoff is precluded by the bankruptcy act. This left a favorable witness with the creditors in spite of the former failures.

11. What's your comment to this?

If or when we fail, especially when it is clearly our own fault, we should not expect that surely *someone else* will pay for our losses or misfortune.

Sometimes one brings things on themselves, and one cannot just turn the page and make it go away. It must be faced and reckoned with. Sometimes people who have failed expect that their relatives or their church will come running to bail them out of their troubles and spare them any inconvenience or discomfort. It certainly is in order for Christians to be compassionate and to help those who have run into trouble. However, it is just as true that there are times when those who get into trouble by acting on their own choices are better off if they are allowed to struggle and to find their own answers for the situation they have created. They might thereby learn some valuable lessons. Might this be some of the meaning of the verse that says "every man shall bear his own burden" (Gal. 6:5)?

12. How shall onlookers decide whether or not to bail someone out?
13. What can parents do for their children to keep them from growing into adults with a *pity me, pay me* approach to failure?

Not all apparent success is ordered by God, and not all perceived failure is a sign of wrong. God "maketh his sun to rise on the evil and on the good, and sendeth rain on the just and on the unjust" (Matt. 5:45). Floods, fire and storms disrupt the life of righteous people as well as the lives of those who are not living by God's rules.

14. Is it easy to quickly pass wrong and unfair judgment?
15. Can the person who is actually at fault and accountable for his failure erroneously use the foregoing scripture and thoughts as a justification of their situation?

When things go wrong, for whatever reason, a good attitude to strive for is recorded in Habakkuk 3:17-18: "Although the fig tree shall not blossom, neither shall fruit be in the vines; the labour of the olive shall fail, and the fields shall yield no meat; the flock shall be cut off from the fold, and there shall be no herd in the stalls: Yet I will rejoice in the Lord, I will joy in the God of my salvation."

16. Is it possible to be so committed to the Lord and so securely trusting in God's provision that failure will not get one down?
17. Is it okay to be more joyful when the going is good than when things do not turn out right?

Insurance and Safekeeping

CHAPTER 22

"Except the Lord keep the city, the watchman waketh but in vain" (Ps. 127;1-b). Many other verses in the Bible hold out that same thought that if the Lord removes His protecting hand, no one is secure.

1. If that is the case, is there any measurable security in insurance?

Other scriptures indicate that it is in order for a steward to keep the city walls repaired and the gates closed at night. The King James Version of the Bible has more than 300 references to gates. While doors and gates do not shield one from all possible trouble, closing the doors and the gates does serve as a deterrent to trouble, theft and sabotage, etc.

The businessmen (or the homeowner) should close the door and, especially depending on where you live, turn the lock to remove the invitation for problems. But don't be fretful or overly concerned about protecting your possessions on the earth.

Endeavoring to lessen the chances of thievery or vandalism is one issue; accepting and coping with what God allows or suffering losses by acts of God is another matter. In relation to these things, consider Job, who said, "The Lord gave and the Lord took" (Job 1:21-22).

Trust and faith in God go a long way toward eliminating the need for insurance. "And call upon me in the day of trouble: I will deliver thee, and thou shalt glorify me" (Ps. 50:15).

2. So, who needs insurance and when? Why? What kind? How much?

3. Do you know any answers for the above questions?
4. On what are you basing your answers?
5. Do you have more insurance than you are required to have?
6. If yes, why?
7. Is it okay for a Christian to accept a life insurance policy required by a bank loan?
8. Does insurance reduce the need of trust in the Lord?

Following are a number of additional scriptures concerning our real security, to whatever degree that it actually exists on this earth.

"The horse is prepared against the day of battle: but safety is of the Lord" (Prov. 21:31).

"Behold, he that keepeth Israel shall neither slumber nor sleep. The Lord is thy keeper: the Lord is thy shade upon thy right hand" (Ps. 121:4-5).

"And we know that all things work together for good to them that love God, to them who are the called according to his purpose" (Rom. 8:28).

"Casting all your care upon him (the Lord); for he careth for you" (1 Pet. 5:7).

"Thus saith the Lord; Cursed be the man that trusteth in man, and maketh flesh his arm, and whose heart departeth from the Lord. For he shall be like the heath in the desert, and shall not see when good cometh; but shall inhabit the parched places in the wilderness, in a salt land and not inhabited. Blessed is the man that trusteth in the Lord, and whose hope the Lord is" (Jer. 17:5-7).

9. To what degree then should a person just relax in confidence in the Lord?
10. Does the quote from Jeremiah apply directly to the insurance issue?

An insurance salesman visited a Christian farmer one day. He asked the farmer to bring out his existing insurance policy so they could compare it with what he had to offer. The farmer readily obliged and soon returned with his Bible. He opened it to Psalm 91 and began reading the promises of God's protection. According to the story, after listening to the reading, the salesman closed his books, and said, "I cannot match that one."

11. Read Psalm 91. Does it still apply in the New Testament era?
12. How does the scripture from Romans 8:28 apply to the insurance question?
13. What part does trust in God and a lack of worry have to do with a proper Christian testimony in the area of insurance and locks, etc.?

Do not worry, God is not handicapped. "Behold, the Lord's hand is not shortened, that it cannot save; neither his ear heavy, that it cannot hear" (Isa. 59:1). If, however, one is in trouble, and God is not helping, it may be due to sin at the door. Verse 2 of the same chapter goes on to say, "But your iniquities have separated between you and your God, and your sins have hid his face from you, that he will not hear."

14. How do these verses in Isaiah 59 affect the insurance question?

Regardless of our understanding of what is proper concerning insurance, there are practical things that can minimize the potential of loss or calamity. Carry out preventive maintenance and exercise caution to avoid losses by fire, accident, or theft, etc. Use common sense practices to reduce fire hazards or other problem points. Properly placing fire extinguishers, fences, lights, and locks; returning things to their proper storage places; avoiding undue risks; and many other such actions can limit the potential of loss and disappointment.

Proverbs 22:3 speaks about preventive actions: "A prudent man foreseeth the evil, and hideth himself: but the simple pass on, and are punished."

15. Can too much thought about preventive measures become a source of worry?
16. How and from what type of evil can the prudent man hide himself?

Liability insurance is a specific area of deliberation about the insurance questions. Sometimes it is a legal requirement for certain circumstances, and sometimes a need for it is only a perception. Insurance companies often imply a need for it to protect one from losing their assets in a lawsuit. To a certain degree lawsuits and their associated injustices are closely connected to questions about a need for insurance. Because of these and other similar things, questions remain about the legitimacy or actual necessity of liability and other insurances.

17. Some people assert that they have liability insurance for the good or protection of the other person. Does it work that way?
18. Would it be better for Christians to shy away from occupations or businesses that require one to be heavily insured by multiple policies?

Incorporating a business or forming a limited liability company (LLC) is another form of insurance. Many people do this mainly for protection against the loss of business or personal assets.

19. Is this a good idea? Is it just a matter of personal choice or opinion?
20. Some view it as good stewardship if you do it with a good attitude. Can it be that?
21. Are self-protection measures always selfish at the root?

Many people buy insurance because of three issues: fear, worry, and selfishness. Some people just about buy themselves poor with all types of insurance, and yet they are anxious about losing their possessions and are otherwise fearful and worried.

22. Can insurance give one any legitimate peace of mind?

There are many types of insurance that are supposed to eliminate worry and make us feel secure. There are diverse self-defensive legal provisions intended to protect people from harm and suffering. If we could view these things from the end of our life, they would likely seem unimportant and perhaps totally useless to the sincere Christian.

23. Do you agree with the foregoing thought?
24. If you do, can you share your explanations or some applicable experiences?

Beware of insurance fraud. There are many types of false claims and misrepresentations used to secure unfair, unethical, or out-right unlawful gains from insurance claims. It is a form of extortion. Conscientious insurance agents call it simple greed. Due to the fallibility of man, this can even show up in church-aid and other sharing plans.

25. Is this type of fraud always motivated by selfishness or greed and always wrong?
26. What safeguards can we implement to deliver us from such temptations?

There is real beauty in church-sponsored aid plans designed to share burdens resulting from losses and help those in need because of misfortune or sickness. This reduces the perceived need of insurance.

There is much value in people standing together and being willing to help each other out in trouble or need. Ecclesiastes 4:9-12 says, "Two *are* better than one.... For if they fall, the one will lift up his fellow: but woe to him that is alone when he falleth; for he hath not another to help him up. Again, if two lie together, then they have heat: but how can one be warm alone? And if one prevail against him, two shall withstand him; and a threefold cord is not quickly broken."

27. Many forms of insurance have been proclaimed to have much value, and sometimes participation is a legal requirement. Has that weakened faith and trust in the Lord for daily protection and help in the time of trouble?
28. Has it weakened the sense of care for one another among Christians?

Coping with Injustice and Lawsuits

CHAPTER 23

Injustice among people is probably as old as the human race. Lawsuits are also not just a modern-day problem. These facts are evident by all the teaching in the Bible about the subject. Injustice happens among all classes and economic circumstances. However, lawsuits appear to be a bigger problem in more affluent societies.

There may be varied views about some of the thoughts and questions that follow. Be prepared and willing to share your input or questions.

COATS, CLOAKS, AND STOLEN GOODS

"Ye have heard that it hath been said, An eye for an eye, and a tooth for a tooth: But I say unto you, That ye resist not evil: but whosoever shall smite thee on thy right cheek, turn to him the other also. And if any man will sue thee at the law, and take away thy coat, let him have thy cloak also. And whosoever shall compel thee to go a mile, go with him twain" (Matt. 5:38-41).

"But I say unto you which hear, Love your enemies, do good to them which hate you, Bless them that curse you, and pray for them which despitefully use you. And unto him that smiteth thee on the one cheek offer also the other; and him that taketh away thy cloak forbid not to take thy coat also. Give to every man that asketh of thee; and of him that taketh away thy goods ask them not again. And as ye would that men should do to you, do ye also to them likewise. For if ye love them which love you, what thank have ye? for sinners also love those that love them. And if ye do good to them which do good to you, what thank have ye? for sinners also do even the same. And if ye lend to them of whom ye hope to receive, what thank have ye? for sinners also lend to sinners, to receive as much again. But love ye your enemies, and do good, and lend, hoping for nothing again; and your reward shall be great, and ye shall be the children of the Highest: for he is kind unto the unthankful and to the evil. Be ye therefore merciful, as your Father also is merciful" (Luke 6:27-36).

"Therefore if thine enemy hunger, feed him; if he thirst, give him drink: for in so doing thou shalt heap coals of fire on his head. Be not overcome of evil, but overcome evil with good" (Rom. 12:20-21).

1. Is the standard held forth in these verses actually attainable, or will we always fall short?
2. Does this mean that we should be helpless and defenseless puppets?
3. What! Even feed the enemy?
4. Can you share any real-life examples of the foregoing scriptures in practice?

GOING TO COURT

"Dare any of you, having a matter against another, go to law before the unjust, and not before the saints? [2]Do ye not know that the saints shall judge the world? and if the world shall be judged by you, are ye unworthy to judge the smallest matters? [3]Know ye not that we shall judge angels? how much more things that pertain to this life? [4]If then ye have judgments of things pertaining to this life, set them to judge who are least esteemed in the church. [5]I speak to your shame. Is it so, that there is not a wise man among you? no, not one that shall be able to judge between his brethren? [6]But brother goeth to law with brother, and that before the unbelievers. [7]Now therefore there is utterly a fault among you, because ye go to law one with another. Why do ye not rather take wrong? why do ye not rather suffer yourselves to be defrauded? [8]Nay, ye do wrong, and defraud, and that your brethren" (1 Cor. 6:1-6).

This scripture appears to be speaking primarily about problems within the Christian brotherhood. The teaching is clear that these problems shall be solved within the brotherhood and not in a courtroom. It also tells us that instead of going to court we should rather be willing to be defrauded.

1. Concerning this issue, is there any difference at all between a fellow church member and anyone else?
2. *Dare any of you* file a lien on someone's property?

"Agree with thine adversary quickly, whiles thou art in the way with him; lest at any time the adversary deliver thee to the judge, and the judge deliver thee to the officer, and thou be cast into prison" (Matt. 5:25). These are the words of Jesus.

In today's language we would say, if at all possible, reach a settlement or agreement with your adversary quickly while you are still able to negotiate, and do whatever you can to stay out of the courtroom. If this is done in humility, you can many times avoid much bigger problems.

3. Is negotiating for sure acceptable, or should one just agree with whatever the demand is?
4. Is any haggling in the negotiating process okay?
5. If all else fails and a Christian is drawn into court, should he hire an attorney to represent him?

In Matthew 10:16, Jesus said, "I send you forth as sheep in the midst of wolves: be ye therefore wise as serpents, and harmless as doves."

6. Does this apply to staying out of courtrooms?
7. If so, how? Can you give an example?

Following are several Scriptures that give us direction for how to attain and maintain peace even though there is much trouble in the world and the times that we live in.

"Let him eschew evil, and do good; let him seek peace, and ensue it, For the eyes of the Lord are over the righteous, and his ears are open unto their prayers" (1 Pet. 3:11-12).

"When a man's ways please the Lord, he maketh even his enemies to be at peace with him. Better is a little with righteousness than great revenues without right" (Prov. 16:7-8).

"Dearly beloved, avenge not yourselves, but rather give place unto wrath: for it is written, Vengeance *is* mine; I will repay, saith the Lord" (Rom. 12:19).

Hebrews 10:34 speaks of some who "took joyfully the spoiling of their goods."

All of these verses have the same tenor: seek the way of peace and allow the Lord to settle matters as He sees best. Never retaliate against those who mistreat you. If you do, you will most likely get the biggest hurt. Let God take care of it. He will do the repaying.

8. So then, how does Matthew 10:13 apply to this subject?
9. How does it work for the Lord to make one's enemies to be at peace with him?
10. If you are at peace with them, can they still be enemies?
11. Can you give an explanation or an example of joyfully taking the spoiling of one's goods?

First Peter 2:19-21 concludes this subject nicely: "For this is thankworthy, if a man for conscience toward God endure grief, suffering wrongfully. For what glory is it, if, when ye be buffeted for your faults, ye shall take it patiently? But if, when ye do well, and suffer for it, ye take it patiently, this is acceptable with God. For even hereunto were ye called: because Christ also suffered for us, leaving us an example, that ye should follow his steps."

Warnings about Envy, Jealousy, Greed, and Covetousness, Etc.

CHAPTER 24

The words of the title sound bad and will do great damage to oneself and to those around the person that is overcome by these negative traits. It is true that God is merciful and does not always reward people according to their iniquity, but normally we do reap what we sow.

Following are scriptures that explain some of the harmful effects of yielding to these negative characteristics.

ENVY

"A sound heart is the life of the flesh: but envy the rottenness of the bones" (Prov. 14:30).

"Wrath *is* cruel, and anger is outrageous; but who is able to stand before envy?" (Prov. 27:4).

JEALOUSY

"For jealousy is the rage of a man" (Prov. 6:34).

"Jealousy is cruel as the grave: the coals thereof are coals of fire, which hath a most vehement flame" (Song of Sol. 8:6).

GREED

"For their feet run to evil, and make haste to shed blood. So are the ways of everyone that is greedy of gain; which taketh away the life of the owners thereof" (Prov. 1:16-19).

"He that is greedy of gain troubleth his own house" (Prov. 15:27).

COVETOUSNESS

"Take heed, and beware of covetousness: for a man's life consisteth not in the abundance of the things which he possesseth" (Luke 12:15).

"Mortify therefore your members which are upon the earth; (a list of things follows) . . . and covetousness, which is idolatry" (Col. 3:5).

Many other scriptures have direct and indirect instruction about these issues and encourage us to be converted from within, so we can indeed "overcome evil with good" (Rom. 12:21).

Greed will dim a person's spiritual vision and common sense, and make one gullible and susceptible to scams of various types. It increases a person's likelihood of being cheated in fraudulent business. Further, it weakens the resolve and wisdom to keep you from participating in unfair or unwise business ventures or programs.

1. "What shall it profit a man, if he shall gain the whole world, and lose his own soul?" (Mark 8:36)
2. Suppose you would accomplish all that you aspire to do and acquire. When you arrive at the end of life's road, what then?
3. Is triumph over greed a matter of personal choice?

"Let your conversation (*your talk and your walk of life*) be without covetousness and be content" (Heb. 13:5).

4. Is the absence of covetousness automatically contentment?
5. Can they ever co-exist?

Even though God often blesses the efforts of those who live uprightly, prosperity is not necessarily a sign, or a result of righteousness. There are many ungodly people who become prosperous and rich. Keep your guard up, so you do not envy the prosperity of the wicked. In Psalm 73, Asaph wrote about his struggle and conclusion on this matter in verse 22. "So foolish was I, and ignorant," he said. Turn to it and read the whole Psalm.

If you become aware that you have a wrong mind-set about this subject, do what the psalmist wrote in Psalm 119:58-60: "I entreated thy favour with my whole heart: be merciful unto me according to thy word. I thought on my ways, and turned my feet unto thy testimonies. I made haste, and delayed not to keep thy commandments."

6. What anchor will keep the Christian on the straight and narrow road as he observes enticing things going on around him, seemingly more desirable than his own circumstances?
7. Is a special kind of anchor required when it appears that some who have everything going for them are not even Christians?

Do not fall in love with the world and the things of the world. This certainly includes an obsession for items of modern technology as well as a passion for antiques and other earthly things. According to 1 John 2:15, misplaced love blocks out the love for the Father: "Love not the world, neither the things that are in the world. If any man love the world, the love of the Father is not in him."

8. What type of love of the world is this speaking about?
9. Can a Christian love the world just a little bit?
10. Does modern technology make this temptation worse?

The Bible says that riches are deceitful. "And the cares of this world, and the deceitfulness of riches, and the lusts of other things entering in, choke the word, and it becometh unfruitful" (Mark 4:19).

11. What is meant by *riches* as used in this verse?
12. How does this deception of riches work? Can you give an example?
13. Considering the scope of this verse, is there any spiritual and social merit or protection in trying to live with the absolute minimum of possessions and involvements?
14. If you think so, can you name any advantages, and how would they be evident?

Mark 10:17-27 tells about a certain young man who became sorrowful at the mere thought of parting with his possessions. He became sad just thinking about it; he had not gotten rid of a single thing yet.

15. Does this potential snare become a greater danger as our holdings increase?

A covetous attitude and pride can seriously hinder God's blessing on a person's financial endeavors. The prodigal son (Luke 15) is an example of calamity because of a wrong mind-set about money. He demanded of his father, *Give me . . . I want it now . . . !* Apparently he could have enjoyed a blessed circumstance had he not demanded his own imprudent desires. Instead of a blessing, he suffered dire consequences.

Many people with a desire to be rich and a love for money have pierced themselves through with sorrows. See 1 Timothy 6:9-11. It doesn't say that they were rich but that they *desired* to be rich.

16. Does this mean one should never desire to advance financially?
17. Can you explain the piercing effect?

Without God, it is often true, as the saying goes; that *much wants more.* A love for silver and abundance will not be satisfied with silver and abundance (Eccl. 5:10). In other words, no amount of holdings or net worth is a pinnacle of achievement that brings automatic contentment and happiness.

Another important concept is in these words of Jesus: "Take heed, and beware of covetousness: for a man's life consisteth not in the abundance of the things which he possesseth" (Luke 12:15).

18. What is the problem when, as someone has said, some people (sometimes even Christians), are like a horse that's standing knee-deep in grass but reaching over the fence to eat?
19. Does this insinuate that covetousness is a result of mistaken thinking about the value of things?
20. The above scripture tells us what life does not consist of. What then, does the spiritual person's life consist of?

Ecclesiastes 5:12 says, "The sleep of a labouring man is sweet, whether he eat little or much: but the abundance of the rich will not suffer him to sleep."

21. Is it the amount of riches or the mind-set that doesn't allow him to sleep?

Matthew 6:19-20 says, "Lay not up for yourselves treasures upon earth, where moth and rust doth corrupt, and where thieves break through and steal: But lay up for yourselves treasures in heaven, where neither moth nor rust doth corrupt, and where thieves do not break through nor steal." Then Proverbs 13:22 says, "A good man leaveth an inheritance to his children's children."

22. Is this a contradiction? If you don't think so, what is your explanation?
23. Is it acceptable for parents to hope they can leave an abundant inheritance or to wish they could be leaving more for their family?
24. Could it be that earthly holdings are not treasures for the sincere Christian?
25. Should a person ever do certain things specifically with the thought of laying up treasures in Heaven?
26. May a person be conscious of the balance of their heavenly treasure account?

Few if any Christian people come to the end of life and wish they had spent more time and effort in material pursuits. After all, in the end, what good would it be to have gained ownership of "the whole world" and to be lost in eternity? (Mark 8:36).

27. Should Christians ever, under any circumstances, come to the end of life and say they should have worked harder to accumulate more?

James 4:3 describes a problem with a different slant than the title of this chapter. It appears people were asking for things and did not receive them "because ye ask amiss, that ye may consume it upon your lusts." They asked for whatever they wanted, to use it for wrong desires and activities.

28. Should one always seriously consider his motives and attitudes before asking the Lord for things?

Sweepstakes, which promise big winnings, work because of greed and covetousness and man's desire to be rich, but they are a source of many piercing sorrows. Most big sweepstakes or lottery winners end up in ruin. Nearly all people know that, at least to a degree, but they still want to win. Keep an ample-sized trash can close to where you sort your mail so you can promptly discard this and all other junk mail.

29. How can a person resist when they sound so enticing and so promising?
30. Don't you think God has better ways to bless his people?
31. What is there to say about door prizes, etc. at business meetings, home merchandise parties and the likes?

Lottery tickets of all types are in the same category and from the same foundation as sweepstakes. Lotteries and gambling can have such an addictive effect that people can be quite poor and yet spend their money on lottery tickets. They do not belong in the Christian's budget.

32. Why do lotteries and similar things succeed in the first place?
33. What makes these things so addicting for many people?

Psalm 121 has a cluster of promises about being preserved from evils. That would surely include the evils addressed in this chapter, as well as all other evils in the world. The Psalm in not lengthy; read it before you discuss the following question.

34. What is the requirement for being sheltered by the protections promised?

One more thought about money and things: *Money is a good servant but a poor master*. The same is true for credit cards. Your money can be your servant or it can become your master. It can be either your tool or a shackle. Which it will be depends nearly totally on you and the choices you make.

Romans 6:13-14 speaks about being dominated by wrong things, and then verse 16 says, "Know ye not, that to whom ye yield yourselves servants to obey, his servants ye are to whom ye obey." Then chapter 12, verse 21 says, "Be not overcome of evil, but overcome evil with good." This should help us to keep money and things from becoming our ruler.

35. What are some illustrations of *good, overcoming* activities that help one to surmount the evils of misplaced values about earthly things?

Retirement and the Sunset Years

CHAPTER 25

The term *sunset years* refers to the years leading up to the end of one's time on the earth. Although people's experiences of aging vary greatly, old age does not need to carry a curse of uselessness. In the natural sense, sunsets are often beautiful, though they occur just before dark. In certain ways this should also be true of Christian people. Following are several scriptures that are not necessarily direct teaching about retirement, but they do relate to the life of older folks.

- "Rebuke not an elder, but entreat him as a father" (1 Tim. 5:1).
- "The hoary head is a crown of glory, if it be found in the way of righteousness" (Prov. 16:31).
- "With the ancient is wisdom; and in length of days understanding. With him is wisdom and strength, he hath counsel and understanding" (Job 12:12-13).

1. Is every older Christian man to be considered as an elder?
2. Can you explain the *crown of glory* mentioned in the scripture from Proverbs?
3. Is it automatically so, as the scripture from Job implies; are older folks as a rule wiser and more understanding than younger people?

In the fall of the year deciduous trees and shrubs put on a pleasing display of color and beauty as summer ends. Then often the leaves flutter and float down gracefully as dormancy and winter set in. There are also flowers that bloom profusely as fall sets in.

4. Are there, or should there be, social and personality similarities to these natural occurrences as people, especially Christian people, age?
5. If so, is it a matter of choice?
6. Could the falling leaves also be likened to willingly relinquishing our earthly holdings as we come toward the end of our lives?
7. Are there any secrets for how to do this gracefully, like a gently falling leaf?

"Those that be planted in the house of the Lord shall flourish in the courts of our God. They shall still bring forth fruit in old age; they shall be fat and flourishing" (Ps. 92:13-14).

Concerning being fruitful even in old age, it is often evident that those aging people who endeavor to stay disciplined and usefully occupied in some way usually fare better in mind and body than those who retire and sit down.

8. How do you understand the term *fat and flourishing*?
9. What are some examples of being usefully occupied and fruitful for aging people?
10. How does it work that those who stay active and occupied tend to stay healthier in body and mind as they age?

An important part of being a senior is to be willing to do some practical grandparenting. Grandparents often have opportunities to be a somewhat neutral sounding board or an unthreatening confidant for their grandchildren. For some this may be more natural than others, but in life *there's something for all to do*. Even if you don't have grandchildren of your own, there are often many ways to serve as a grandparent to others. Those who take interest and time for this, play an important role in beautifying the human scene.

11. How mindful should grandparents be about not spoiling their grandchildren?
12. Should it be natural for grandparents to have the confidence of their grandchildren?
13. Is there much danger of grandparents getting in the way of the parents and causing more difficulty than they help?

14. What should parents do if they think their parents are overzealous in their involvements as grandparents?

Do your best not to arrive at sunset with unresolved problems and an unfulfilled life. Endeavor to grow old gracefully.

"But speak thou the things which become sound doctrine: That the *aged men* be sober, grave, temperate, sound in faith, in charity, in patience. The *aged women* likewise, that they be in behaviour as becometh holiness, not false accusers, not given to much wine, teachers of good things" (Titus 2:1-3).

15. Does it take a special grace to attain the qualities listed in these verses?
16. How much does personal resolve have to do with it?

"When thou wast young, thou girdedst thyself, and walkedst whither thou wouldest: but *when thou shalt be old,* thou shalt stretch forth thy hands, and another shall gird thee, and carry thee whither thou wouldest not" (John 21:18). This is a fact of old age for many people. Many have to surrender to the care of other people, and some of it may not be to their liking.

17. Are there any special secrets for older people to learn that will make them better able to accept necessary help?
18. How much or in what way should children hear and honor the personal wishes of their aged and perhaps helpless parents?

The need for trust in God and reliance on His promises continues on into old age. Frequently as people age they tend to feel less secure, and some experience an increased tendency to worry. The following scriptures should relieve fears.

- "And they that know thy name will put their trust in thee: for thou, Lord, hast not forsaken them that seek thee" (Ps. 9:10).
- "I have been young, and now am old; yet have I not seen the righteous forsaken, nor his seed begging bread" (Ps. 37:25).
- "For the Lord will not cast off his people, neither will he forsake his inheritance" (Ps. 94:19).
- "And we know that all things work together for good to them

that love God, to them who are the called according to *his* purpose" (Rom. 8:28).

- "Let your conversation be without covetousness; and be content with such things as ye have: for he hath said, I will never leave thee, nor forsake thee" (Heb. 13:5).

19. Whether you are young or older, do any of the above scriptures have a special meaning for you?
20. Can you name some practical things that children and grandchildren should or should not do to help their parents feel secure and provided for?
21. As parents age, they can become more dependent, possibly insecure, and perhaps even disoriented. Is there anything children can do in preparation for this time so they can meet their needs with a good attitude and not get frustrated?

Proverbs 23:22-25 instructs children about their attitude toward their aging parents. "Hearken unto thy father that begat thee, and despise not thy mother *when she is old*. Buy the truth, and sell it not; also wisdom, and instruction, and understanding. The father of the righteous shall greatly rejoice: and he that begetteth a wise child shall have joy of him. Thy father and thy mother shall be glad, and she that bare thee shall rejoice" (Prov. 23:22-25).

Although 1 Timothy 5:3-16 is primarily about the welfare of widows in need, verse four says that children or nephews should, "learn first to show piety at home, and to requite (*or repay*) their parents: for that is good and acceptable before God." Because the term *nephews* is used with children, it appears that responsibility is not limited only to one's own parents but could include uncles, aunts and perhaps grandparents.

22. To what degree then may parents expect their children or other relatives to support and care for them in their aged years?
23. The scripture above mentions nephews; what about nieces?

Preparing for Your Departure

CHAPTER 26

"To everything there is a season, and a time to every purpose under the heaven: A time to be born, and a time to die" (Eccl. 3:1-2). In the normal course of earthly life there is the season to be up and doing, and then life progresses to the season for departure. Whatever the season in life, it should be the Christian's goal to always be prepared for departure.

Even though this chapter is close to the end of the book, do not wait to the end of your life to consider the facts of this chapter. When the questions about eternity are satisfied, and you are inwardly prepared to die, then you are ready to live. Too many people, however, are too busy living to have time to think much about their departure.

Remember: we are not here to stay. This truth is well documented by many scriptures, and observation proves that death is as certain as birth. The scripture says, "It is appointed unto men once to die, but after this the judgment" (Heb. 9:27). The vast majority of people do not know ahead of time when their appointment is. So it's very important to live now the way you want to die and the way you would like to be remembered after you are gone.

Another somewhat surprising scripture says, "It is better to go to the house of mourning, than to go to the house of feasting: for that is the end of all men; and the living will lay it to his heart" (Eccl. 7:2).

1. How can we best keep our end in mind without worrying or living in fear or bewilderment?
2. What does it mean that the living will lay it (the definite end of man) to his heart?

In Philippians 1:21 the Apostle Paul says, "For to me to live is Christ, and to die is gain."

3. God has made people with a desire to stay alive. Why then would anyone say that to die is gain?

In the Old Testament, Hezekiah was given a definite message about his imminent death. "In those days was Hezekiah sick unto death. And the prophet Isaiah, the son of Amoz, came to him and said unto him, Thus saith the Lord, *Set thine house in order*; for thou shalt die, and not live" (2 Kings 20:1).

4. What kind of setting in order do you think Hezekiah was supposed to do?
5. Do you think he had bad business deals to correct, overdue borrowed things to return, or was he just being encouraged to record a will?

We all came with nothing, and it is certain we're all leaving that same way. See 1 Timothy 6:7. The certain rich man in Luke 12:14-20 was told, you will die tonight, then whose will these things be?

When you go, you will leave everything here, regardless of who you are, what you are, or what you have. The wise and the fool leave alike! See Psalm 49:10. What then?

6. As you grow older, or realize for another reason that the time of your departure is drawing close, will you be able to lay your things down, or will they need to be torn from you?
7. How can one be prepared and willing to *let go* of earthly things.
8. Can we know the answer to these questions ahead of time?

The most pressing need of preparation for our departure is finding forgiveness for our sins and peace with God. Assuming that your spiritual need is satisfied, we will consider some practical things that pertain to preparation for departing from the earthly life.

Making a will (or testament) was an accepted and perhaps expected practice already in Bible times. Some scriptures that refer to this are Job 42:15b, Luke 12:13-15 and Hebrews 9:16-17.

Many people have said something like, Well, what do I care what happens with my stuff after I am gone? In one sense this is a noble attitude. Yet, in another sense, it is irresponsible because if you pass away without a will, it will be more difficult for your survivors and heirs to settle your affairs. Drawing up a will is an important part of setting one's house in order. It will make things easier for your spouse or children and others left behind.

9. It is said that drawing up a will is one of the most common areas of procrastination. Why is this?
10. Does an unwillingness to leave or a fear of death cause people to procrastinate in making preparations for departure?

Following are some items to consider in making or updating a will.

- A small booklet, *Christian Stewardship in Estate Planning*, is available from Gospel Publishers to help plan a will. Advice and counsel from knowledgeable people is also helpful. If you have access to it, read the Stewardship article about this subject in the *Messenger of Truth*, Volume 105, No. 5, February 28, 2007. There are many instruction books available about the subject.
- The welfare of your minor children is an important issue. Choose a guardian for them. Even though laws vary from state to state and in different countries, yet do the best you can to make it easier for those left behind to take care of your family.
- Teach your children the right values now, so they will not fight for your possessions after you are gone. Far too often children seem to get along fine, but when their parents die, many have problems settling the estate. Parents should be able to help their children avoid future problems concerning this issue by giving them the right training as children.
- Endeavor to maintain a proper understanding and mind-set of these matters as you and your children grow older.
- Think beyond your family and also give back to the Lord; name His church and charitable organizations among your beneficiaries.

Some years ago a now-deceased minister shared his observations and deep concern about this issue. He was determined to do what he could to spare his children from skirmishing when the time came to settle the estate. After his passing one of the children stated that their parents had things well defined and properly communicated, and that they had no problems settling the estate. It was a commendable testimony.

Beware of the selfish thought of deliberately giving all your assets to your children, so they can live fine and first-rate, and then relying on the government, (really your fellow taxpayers) to support and take care of you in your old age. Currently, in the U.S. this is viewed by the government as an unfair practice. Therefore they have provided a legal way to reach back a certain number of years in an effort to reclaim funds given to the children (or other heirs) during that time frame.

11. Should children be able to cheerfully watch their parents use up their assets for their old-age care?

Today's increased holdings, higher real-estate values, and greater lifestyle involvement make dispersing one's goods and property more complex than in the past. Finding workable ways to scale down as a couple ages can be a bit difficult. However, leaving too much to be dispersed increases the potential of disputes and can cause lots of problems for family members.

12. What should you or your parents do or not do about these facts?

When people were spelling out their will in the Old Testament times they were not allowed to sidestep common practice in favor for a more-beloved heir. See Deuteronomy 21:15-17.

13. Does this principle concerning favoritism hold true in the New Testament era?

Deuteronomy 21:15-17 indicates that the oldest son was given special advantages. In more recent times among many people the youngest son was the one to be given special benefits.

14. Does it matter one way or the other, or should it be neither?

The Scripture does not require parents to leave an inheritance, large or small, for their children. What is important is to leave proper teaching and a good example of consecration to the Lord and His will. This is of more value than an inheritance. It has the potential of producing far-reaching good effects for generations to come, if time continues that long.

It might be right for some people, as they approach the end of life, to regret that they did not apply themselves more diligently to provide better for themselves and their families.

15. If that is the case, what, if anything, can they do about it?
16. Is it fair for parents who need support in their old age to expect their children to support them or at least to help?

Your spouse should have complete knowledge of your preparations for departure and of the location of legal documents and other important papers, etc. Someone else in your family should also have at least some knowledge of the same.

17. Where and how should wills and other legal or important documents be stored?

To summarize preparations for departure: Live prepared to die, and be ready for your call and alert for the coming of the bridegroom! See Matthew 24:42 and 25:6.

18. Is funeral pre-planning a good idea?

Endeavor to live so that when your day for departure draws near, you can say with Paul, "For I am now ready to be offered, and the time of my departure is at hand. I have fought a good fight, I have finished my course, I have kept the faith: Henceforth there is laid up for me a crown of righteousness, which the Lord, the righteous judge, shall give me at that day: and not to me only, but unto all them also that love his appearing" (2 Tim. 4:6-8).

Facing the Future

CHAPTER 27

In the beginning of this study we considered the thought from Matthew 6:30-34 about "seeking first the kingdom of God," and from Luke 16:10-12 about being "faithful in that which is least." These scriptures should incite us to endeavor to live faithfully so we can depart saved and in peace.

Many subjects have been addressed in this course. Not everything is of equal importance, and not everything applies to all people. However, now you will have to decide what you will do with whatever God may have spoken to you about in the course of this study.

1. Considering the various subjects and what the Scriptures say about them, what do you think is the secret for being faithful and diligent with your earthly things without getting caught up in materialism or being overcharged with the cares of this life?
2. What should you do if you seem to be alone in your pursuit of what you understand to be right and good?

Don't stop now. After you close this book, you should continue to daily seek for God's way of wisdom and blessings. The more familiar you are with the right way, the less the chance that you will carelessly or unintentionally drift off course. Become familiar with the ultimate instruction manual, the Bible. It's a tool book for living.

Perhaps every day, or at least when there are decisions to make, take time to stop and think, listen and share, look and watch, study and ask questions. And pray for wisdom. "If any of you lack wisdom, let him ask of God, that giveth to all men liberally, and upbraideth not; and it shall be given him" (James 1:5).

Sharing is important because by open and honest sharing people can be of much help and encouragement to each other. It is also important among fellow church members because ministers and deacons cannot be everywhere all the time. People can do much for each other if they are willing.

3. What can you go by to know what is your place to fill?
4. Why are people so often reluctant or even scared to reach out to help each other along in the challenges of life?
5. What should you do if you offend someone you really meant to help?

To enhance your spiritual sense of direction, listen for the gentle whisper, the still small voice referred to in 1 Kings 19:12, and don't override your spiritual direction. Be careful not to let your conscience get "seared," as mentioned in 1 Timothy 4:2. Another requisite for spiritual success on the earth is in Galatians 5:16: "This I say then, Walk in the Spirit, and ye shall not fulfill the lust of the flesh."

Dress yourself in the whole armor of God that you may be able to withstand the tricks of the devil (Eph. 6:11). Finding the necessary spiritual direction for everyday living has lots to do with common sense.

6. How would you explain a seared conscience?
7. What is *the whole armor*?

Second Timothy 2:3-5 teaches us to endure hardness and not to get entangled with the affairs of this life. This is a delicate subject that through the years has received a wide scope if interpretations. It does not say that we should have nothing and be a recluse or a hermit, but that we should not get entangled (or tied up) with the things of this life.

8. How would you interpret entanglement?
9. Is an effort to run and hide just as far off track as freely blending in with whatever is the current way of life among the public?
10. What are some specific do's or don'ts that relate to being in the world but not of the world?

11. Does a bare-minimum lifestyle afford any safety from entanglement?
12. Could too much emphasis on very simple living actually be a form of selfishness?

Hebrews 12:1 gives more instructions for how to proceed: "Let us lay aside every weight, and the sin which doth so easily beset us, and let us run with patience the race that is set before us." It seems to say that we should travel light as we make our way through our allotted time on the earth.

13. What do you think it means about laying aside *every weight*?
14. In relation to this, consider the questions in Mark 8:36-37 again.

In the early 1900s, among the Mennonites in Lancaster County, Pennsylvania, there lived a man known as Blind Johnny Wenger. Some of this man's experiences serve as natural examples of spiritual truths.

One time when he accomplished something marvelous for a blind man, he was asked, "Johnny, how were you able to do this?" He replied, "Well, we blind people use our brains. The rest of you don't." It is well known that blind people compensate for their lack of eyesight with diligent mental awareness. If all Christians would be more diligent to use their brains and practice spiritual awareness, surely we would fare better in finding our way in life.

For a number of years this Blind Johnny had a retail store. When people entered his place of business, he often knew who it was by the time they closed the door. On one occasion a man who had not been there for a long time decided to visit and see if Blind Johnny still knew him. He entered without speaking. The blind man did not say anything but listened intently. The visitor walked over to the old potbelly stove where he took a seat. As soon as the man sat down, Blind Johnny greeted him by name. Quite naturally the man wanted to know how he knew him. "Well," Johnny said, "whenever you sit down you make a certain soft little grunt." Because Johnny listened carefully, he heard the telltale sign that gave away the man's identity.

So it may be for us when we meet perplexing things in life. If we listen carefully for any telltale signs or sense of direction, we may be able to perceive, as in Isaiah 30:21: "And thine ears shall hear a word behind thee, saying, This is the way, walk ye in it, when ye turn to the right hand, and when ye turn to the left." The voice might be quite *still and small*, but the more carefully we listen, the better our chance of hearing it. The more we discipline ourselves to stop and think, really think and pray, the more likely we will be to find a sense of direction.

And according to Hebrews 5:14, as we practice and exercise ourselves to perceive such godly directions for life, we should become better at it. It talks about people who "by reason of use have their senses exercised to discern both good and evil."

This subject is vital because we live in a time of dire need for a personal spiritual sense of direction. Due to all the modern technology, the fast pace of change, and the pressure from the multitude of necessary decisions, we are facing high-speed, high-tech, and sometimes fiery trials. Although the issues of trials may have changed, difficult trials are not modern-day news. And when complex trials come, we are not supposed to think it strange. See 1 Peter 4:12.

There is also an urgent need for Christians who are willing to be of use to the Lord and their fellowman. This should be with compassion and concern, reaching out with the cup of cold water, and helping others to find the way.

15. Is it possible for Christians to always stay as alert as they should?
16. What can you do if worry or fear strikes you as you seek to find your way?
17. How much should we deliberately think of reaching out to help others?

Endeavor to proceed with joy and peace of mind. There are many scriptures that encourage us to joyful living, and there are many that speak about peace of mind, even though things may not be as we would like. Jesus promised us peace unlike anything in the world. "Peace I leave with you, my peace I give unto you: not as the world giveth, give I unto you. Let not your heart be troubled, neither let it be afraid" (John 14:27).

"Thou wilt show me the path of life: in thy presence is fullness of joy; at thy right hand there are pleasures for evermore" (Ps. 16:11). Any or all of us may have our share of trials and disappointments; "*weeping may endure for a night, but joy cometh in the morning*" (Ps. 30:5-b).

18. What effects will an honest pursuit of godly joy and peace have on how we face the future?
19. Does one need to be somewhat unrealistic or to ignore the facts to experience peace and joy regardless of unfavorable circumstances?

Strive to be wise. Build on the rock. Do the sermon on the mountain. "Therefore whosoever heareth these sayings of mine, and doeth them, I will liken him unto a wise man, which built his house upon a rock: And the rain descended, and the floods came, and the winds blew, and beat upon that house; and it fell not: for it was founded upon a rock" (Matt. 7:24-25).

To receive God's blessing, be a doer of what you know to do. "But whoso looketh into the perfect law of liberty, and continueth therein, he being not a forgetful hearer, but a doer of the work, this man shall be blessed in his deed" (James 1:25). This promise of a blessing is for those who actually make themselves live according to the Bible and the Holy Spirit. To be blessed in their deeds, or we might say to enjoy God's blessing on their way of living, is something of great value to man.

We must always remember though, that God sometimes allows righteous people to suffer in a variety of ways, for reasons of His own that may not be evident to us.

20. How concerned or conscious should we be about whether or not we are *successful doers*?
21. If we are doing what we understand to be right, how much may we expect a blessing for it?

If you think you are not on the right track and need to change the course of your life, be careful. There is a danger in making quick, impulsive or radical moves or changes. Quite often it is a fact that "haste makes waste." Perhaps you will need to make some changes, but don't do it too hastily or in a panic. That increases the chances of making wrong choices.

An honest willingness to change when it is necessary is important though. Far too many people, when a course correction is required, are willing, as long as it doesn't require sacrifice or undesired change. Sometimes necessary changes are a relief, and sometimes, unfortunately, they hurt.

Be wise and humble, and pay serious attention to the wisdom of older, experienced people, even though they may seem overly cautious, or as we say, *from the old school*. Learning from those who have gone before you can be a big help and will give you an increased measure of safety.

22. An old adage says *no pain, no gain*. Is this the way it is with necessary changes for personal and spiritual advancement?
23. In general, should young people be more eager to receive counsel and advice from older folks?

Another thing to help us stay balanced on this earth is what 2 Peter 3:11 says: Knowing that all these things (all our possessions) will be dissolved, what kind of people should we be? A dying father told his son, "Son, do the best you can and the best you know about these earthly things, but just remember that when you get to where I am, all earthly things will mean very little."

24. Is it possible to always remember that?

On U.S. currency it says, "In God We Trust." Do you, for your source of money and for your provisions of life? Trust in anything other than God is bound to let you down. Keep in mind that there is no total security on the earth except in God.

25. It may help to re-read Psalm 91 from time to time.

Proverbs 30:8b-9 records the prayer of a man named Agur: "Give me neither poverty nor riches; feed me with food convenient for me: Lest I be full, and deny thee, and say, Who is the Lord? or lest I be poor, and steal, and take the name of my God in vain."

This is a good ideal for all Christian people. Look for a working balance that is right for you and your family according to Bible principles. Then apply self-discipline to stay on course. If you don't row diligently with the oars of godly wisdom and common sense, your canoe of life will be carried downstream with the currents of society and worldly trends. The right way is upstream and is better than the ways of the world.

26. Can we never relax? Must we always be living on edge, so to speak?

One other thing about living our faith is that we are supposed to pray for the privilege to live a quiet and peaceable life, in all godliness and honesty. This is good and acceptable in the sight of God (1 Tim. 2:1-3).

27. How would you describe an ideal *quiet and peaceable life* for the Christian?

Here are several simple but comforting promises.

"Trust in the Lord, and do good; so shalt thou dwell in the land, and verily thou shalt be fed" (Ps. 37:3). "O fear the Lord, ye his saints: for there is no want to them that fear him" (Ps. 34:9). In other words, worship the Lord, and there will be a way for you, and you will have your needs supplied.

28. Is it really that simple?
29. If so, why do we have to work for a living?

Numbers 6:24-26 has a blessing spoken by Moses to Aaron and his sons: "The Lord bless thee, and keep thee: The Lord make his face shine upon thee, and be gracious unto thee: The Lord lift up his countenance upon thee, and give thee peace."

30. Can we also, yet today attain that blessing?

Don't give up. There is a great prize to be had. "So run, that ye may obtain. And every man that striveth for the mastery is temperate in all things. Now they do it to obtain a corruptible crown; but we an incorruptible" (1 Cor. 9:24-25). And more encouragement follows from Hebrews 12:1: "Let us run with patience the race that is set before us."

This race of faith takes place seven days a week in the everyday things and experiences of life. It is not a matter of the mind that is separate from work or business, or one's lifestyle and social conduct. Someone next to you may give up the race. Do you have what it takes to keep going regardless of what others do?

Remember again the determination of Joshua, who told the people that regardless of what they would do or who they were going to follow, "as for me and my house, we will serve, (*or follow*) the Lord" (Josh. 24:15).

Learn perseverance and proceed with trust and faith. Don't let the fear of failure paralyze you. However, if a course correction is actually necessary, do it.

Turn back now, to page 15 and re-read, "How Do You Live Your Dash?"

So: "*Let us not be weary in well doing: for in due season we shall reap, if we faint not. As we have therefore opportunity, let us do good unto all men, especially unto them who are of the household of faith*" (Gal. 6:9-10).

One's best hope and chance for a good, satisfying life, and for having the necessities of life filled, lies to a large degree in the seriousness of one's faith in God and commitment to His requisites.

A WISE PERSON CHOOSES A DESTINATION AND
ACCEPTS THE WAY;
A FOOL CHOOSES A WAY
AND ACCEPTS THE DESTINATION.

—Anonymous

Which one will you choose?

About the Author

Luke S. Weaver was born in1948, the fourth child in an Old Order Mennonite family of nine. He spent the first part of his childhood on the family farm, in the Berks County German culture of southeastern Pennsylvania. When he was 10 years old, he was afflicted with polio, which left its impact and a slight handicap. He received an elementary education, mostly in the local Mennonite parochial schools.

When Luke's father ventured into business as a hardware and farm supply store owner, he received further education as he followed his father's very practical and sound business principles and work ethics. His father planted strong values of integrity and honesty in his children. He taught things like; "It's not a good deal unless it's good for both the buyer and the seller".

In 1971, while in 1-W Service, he found a new and personal relationship with God, which made profound changes in his attitudes and approach to life. In 1992 he was ordained as a deacon in the Church of God in Christ, Mennonite at Fleetwood, Pa. Life's experiences including those as a business owner, a deacon, and a father of five children, have all been woven into the tapestry of his life, giving him a unique preparation to be the author of this study of Biblical principles of finance and lifestyle.

- Samuel S. Shirk